Europe Is Rising!

Europe Is Rising!

N.W. Hutchings
Joseph Carr
Texe Marrs
J.R. Church
Gary Stearman

— Hearthstone —
—— Publishing ——
— Ltd. —

On the Cover

The picture on the front cover is a reproduction of a poster circulated by the Council of Europe in Brussels, one of the three main divisions of EEC. The poster is a combination of a fifteenth century drawing of the Tower of Babel, with the imposition of a modern crane, illustrating that the Common Market alliance in 1992 will complete the building of a one-world order whose top will reach to Heaven. The twelve stars represent the 1990 membership of the Common Market.

All scripture references are from the King James Version unless otherwise stated

Europe Is Rising!
First Edition, 1990
Copyright © by **Hearthstone Publishing**
Oklahoma City, OK 73101

Printed in the United States of America

Published by:
Hearthstone Publishing
P.O. Box 1144
Oklahoma City, OK 73101

Library of Congress Catalog Card Number 90-81225
ISBN 0-9624517-1-1

Table of Contents

Chapter One

Europe In the New Age

by Texe Marrs

What a difference a year makes! In July 1989, the Berlin Wall was still standing and the communists were in control of Poland, Romania, Czechoslovakia, Hungary, East Germany, and the other countries behind the Iron Curtain. But something very strange and unusual happened in Eastern Europe and the Soviet Union.

Some say that Gorbachev is a savior. Some say this could be the beginning of a great millennium of peace, harmony, justice, love, and brotherhood. However, the Bible gives us a warning in 1 Thessalonians 5:3, *"For when they shall say, Peace and safety; then sudden destruction cometh upon them. . . ."* Daniel tells of a last-days world ruler who will speak dark sentences, meaning he'll know how to manipulate people by lying and by sinister motives (Dan. 8:23). Daniel 8:25 also says that this world ruler, the Antichrist *". . . by peace shall destroy many. . . ."* How can you destroy through peace? Something incredible *is* happening, and I believe that God has told us these things would happen.

The Bible says in Revelation 13 and 17, and

1

Daniel 2, 7, and 9 there will be a world empire in the last days. Could this world empire be forming right now as we read the newspaper headlines each day? Could it be materializing in Europe? What about the Iron Curtain that is coming down, and the Soviet Union? Does all of this mean that the world will have democracy, peace, love, justice, and brotherhood? There must be another side to all these events. They must hold a deeper meaning or significance.

We must realize for many centuries, particularly in the last several decades, a great movement for a one-world order has been taking shape. Many groups, from the World Federalists to the United Nations, are promoting a one-world order. Some have pushed for a one-world, global democratic order. Others really don't care, as long as there is an effective world system, a world government, and a world leader who will ensure that the environment is cleaned, distribution of resources is assured, and the hungry are fed. They are willing to let anyone take over the world if these goals can be achieved.

On June 25-30, 1989, in San Jose, Costa Rica, in Central America, over 700 of the most important New Age leaders met in a conference with politicians, social planners, and religious leaders. They hammered out an agenda for the next decade, the 1990s. I am convinced that the decade leading to the year 2000 will be the most tumultuous, chaotic, and staggering days of our lives. It is very possible that those of us who know Jesus will be viewing these events very soon from Heaven with our Lord Jesus Christ. He will come with a shout, with a trumpet, and we who know Him will be lifted up in the rapture, taken up forcibly to meet the dead in Christ and will be with the Lord forevermore. Then there will be great tribulation on the earth.

What exactly happened in Costa Rica? According to a bulletin by World Goodwill, a major New Age organization founded by Lucius Trust (headquartered jointly in London, Geneva, and New York):

> *"It was a remarkable and historic occasion. There was enthusiastic and generous participation by religious leaders, including the Dalai Lama of Tibetan Buddhism, the Catholic archbishop of San Jose, the government of Costa Rica including President Jose Arias. . . ."*

Jose Arias won the Nobel Peace Prize, a man of great world stature.

> *"There were also representatives of the United Nations. Children there took part in a children's congress."*

What did all these New Age leaders decide? Dr. Robert Muller, former assistant secretary-general of the United Nations, a man who had the vast power of the United Nations in his grasp, stated that what we need by the year 2000 is a one-world religion.

> *"We need a world or a cosmic spirituality. Religious leaders will get together before the end of this century and define the common laws which are common to all their faiths. They will tell the politicians what these cosmic laws are, what God or the gods of the cosmos are expecting from humans."*

He also claims there will be a millennium of integration and harmony of humanity. Muller also said:

> *"Only a one-world political order can set things right. It is time we recognize it."*

There are incredible plans afoot for the next decade before the seventh millennium comes to bring things to a head. I believe Satan is behind these plans and momentous events.

The Bible says this and other amazing things would occur. Take, for example, the events occurring in the Soviet Union. People say that Gorbachev has turned his back on war. He's turned his back on Soviet communism and is ready for the new world order. *Glasnost* means openness, and *perestroika* means to restructure. Has Gorbachev turned his back on the

Stalinist-Leninist past, the death-labor camps, slavery, the mass collectivisation, the monstrous brutality of the communist system? Has he indeed?

Ezekiel 38 and 39 tells of a land led by a leader called Gog in the Bible. According to Ezekiel, Gog is the chief prince of Meshech and Tubal. By researching history, it is easy to document that Meshech means Moscow or Russia, and Tubal is the Russian city of Tobolsk. Ezekiel prophesied God's stance toward Gog in Ezekiel 39:1-2, ". . . *Behold, I am against thee, O Gog, the chief prince of Meshech and Tubal: And I will turn thee back . . . and will cause thee to come up from the north parts, and will bring thee upon the mountains of Israel."* This is phenomenal! God is going to bring Gog back. He's going to turn the Soviet Union around. If Gorbachev fails, his successor will do this. Whatever is happening in the Soviet Union at this time will be reversed so that they will attack Israel. War is not over. We are not assured of world peace because God prophesied that in the last days something else would occur. In Ezekiel 38:4, God says, "*. . . I will turn thee back, and put hooks into thy jaws. . . ."*

Gorbachev may or may not want peace. Personally, I don't trust him, and I'm sorry to say so. Orange County, California, is a bastion of conservative republicanism. Certainly, those people wouldn't trust Mr. Gorbachev very much. But a recent poll showed Gorbachev's credibility received a higher rating than did President George Bush's. Isn't that amazing? A poll taken in West Germany showed that 40 percent trusted George Bush, while 90 percent trusted Mikhail Gorbachev. It is a sad commentary that the people of the world have had the wool pulled over their eyes.

Is Gorbachev really a convert to the ideals of democracy and a free market economy? Former President Richard Nixon may or may not command your respect, but he certainly knows foreign affairs. No one ever accused Richard Nixon of not knowing world and foreign affairs. In *Time* magazine, December 18, 1989, Richard Nixon was asked the same question. What about Gorbachev? Is he really a man of peace? Is he for individual rights, capitalism, and democracy? He said:

"Whoever believes that will believe Santa Claus is bringing my grandchildren the $150 Nintendo set I am buying them for Christmas."

What he is saying is there are evidently those who still believe in Santa Claus. If you believe in Gorbachev, you'll probably believe in Santa Claus, no matter your age. I think Richard Nixon is right about this matter.

An article in a recent edition of *Vanity Fair* magazine described Mikhail Gorbachev's ability to be cunning and clever. It notes that those in the Soviet Union aren't very enthralled with him. The citizens of the Soviet Union cannot be counted among his most ardent supporters. Why have they rioted in Armenia,

Azerbaidzhan, Georgia, and Lithuania? They want freedom from this man. They don't trust him; they don't believe in him. They don't trust in Gog, the chief prince of Meshech and Tubal. Perhaps God has put in their hearts a healthy distrust of this man and the Soviet Communist Party. Perhaps we should have the same distrust.

God said, "... *I will turn thee back, and put hooks into thy jaws* ..." to attack Israel. As events are transpiring in the Soviet Union, to save his neck and restore unity, Gorbachev or his successor could start World War III. To unify Russia and help the Communist Party regain power, or to prevent the collapse of the economy and ease the dire poverty, to bail out the nation, could they possibly go down to the Middle East and as the Bible says, "... *take a spoil* ..." (Ezek. 38:12)? What about the billions of dollars of oil in the Middle East? Would that not put the Soviet economy on a more solid foundation? Wouldn't Israeli technology and Israeli scientists help the Soviet economy a great deal? After World War II, German scientists were forcibly taken to the Soviet Union and made to work as slaves on the atomic bomb and other scientific technology. Might the communists someday do that to Israeli scientists and bring the Israeli technological miracle to the Soviet Union?

As we leave Russia and look into Europe, our speculation is, what is happening in Germany? Amazing events are also taking place there. No one knew a year ago that the Berlin Wall would come tumbling down. No one knew that German people would mingle among themselves, crying out in the streets, arm-in-arm, "Give us a united Germany!" Some are frightened of the prospect of a united Germany. Could a reunited Germany bring about a fourth reich? Is it possible that the fires of World War II could be reignited? One Czechoslovakian leader was quoted in the *New York Times* as saying:

> *"All of Germany's neighbors have got to be against reunification. Once East and West Germany have been unified, what is to stop the Germans from wanting to get back all their old lands in the east, from Pomerania* [part of Poland] *to Silesia* [southwest Poland] *and the Sudeten land* [Czechoslovakia]. *"*

There is much fear in the thought of a reunited Germany, and I believe the rapture clock is ticking today.

Helmut Kohl said of the German nation:

> *"We belong together, and no matter how long it will take, in the end we will achieve the unity and the freedom of Germany."*

I don't question West German Chancellor Helmut Kohl's motives. A satanic book entitled *Maitreya's*

Mission, published by the Share International Foundation, was authored by Benjamin Creme who believes in the New Age false christ, the Lord Maitreya. In the book, Mr. Creme says his spirit guide, the master of Djwhal Khual, has prophesied that:

"Germany will again give the world the blueprint of a correct, that is spiritually-oriented, hierarchical form of government."

Adolf Hitler from Germany offered a blueprint of a hierarchical form of government, and now a demon master is telling this New Age leader it is going to come again.

He also says that Germany's national motto will again be recognized. Isn't it interesting that even a New Age demon spirit knows that Germany's blueprint for the world will be put into action very soon? Can we trust demon spirits? I think not, and I wouldn't give any of this any credence at all if it weren't for the Bible prophesying a great revival of the Roman Empire. Revelation 13 describes a beast with seven heads and ten horns with ten crowns, which are ten kings or kingdoms in the last days. Will they arise up out of a reunited Germany, this great economic power rising from the ashes of World War II today?

Other unusual and incredible developments have recently begun to transpire. The growth of anti-Semitism, a hatred of Jews, is spreading throughout

Germany. Who is causing this? What kind of horror is being raised up in people? The *Washington Post* news service in a report from Berlin states:

> *"Vandalism, death threats, and public demonstrations by neo-Nazis have led East Germany to warn against the rise of neo-fascist groups."*

There are reports that the new Nazis want to have a fourth reich in a united Germany. That should frighten those who don't know Jesus Christ and are wondering what is happening in the world today. In a recent edition of the *Washington Post*, George Will wrote that *perestroika* was the foreign word given the widest usage in the 1980s, but in the 1990s there will be a German word that is coined and used. If 1989 was the year of triumph for freedom, 1990 could possibly be a year of tragedy for the cause of freedom. The dark side of Eastern Europe and Russia could be revealed.

Chapter Two

Was Hitler a Dress Rehearsal for the 1990s?

by Joseph Carr

Adolf Hitler — who was he? What crimes did he commit? Why did he commit those crimes? Could another Adolf Hitler possibly rise to power today? Will that person be the Antichrist, the beast of Revelation 13 in Bible prophecy? What of German reunification? Incredible and momentous events are occurring at this moment throughout Eastern and Western Europe, as well as behind the Iron Curtain in the Soviet Union. Will these culminate in the Antichrist coming to power?

Something very remarkable is happening on the world scene today. If everything that has happened in Europe and the Soviet Union had been accurately predicted at this time last year, no one would have believed any of it. It is so amazing that no reasonable person could have expected it. People want to know the answers to what is happening. The Bible foretold about a revived Roman Empire in the last days, Mystery Babylon, a ten-nation confederation. Considering what is happening in Europe today, without being dogmatic but trying to be realistic, could this be the stirrings of Mystery Babylon? It is important to be cautious on speculative prophecy and to examine the facts carefully, but this does meet the various tests given it. The nations are coming together, and they are in the correct area. This does seem to meet the test of biblical prophecy and is a very strong possibility, but we won't know for certain until the Lord comes. Any reasonable, prudent person who is knowledgeable of the prophecies would say that the present picture of Europe is a strong candidate for a revived Roman Empire.

During the 1930s and 1940s, many thought Adolf Hitler was the Antichrist. Although there is speculation that another Hitler could arise in the 1990s, it is important to learn about the first Hitler. Who was Adolf Hitler, and what crimes did he commit? On one level, he was simply a poor artist who never achieved success in his chosen profession. However, on another scale, he is probably the most demonically-driven dictator of all time. Adolf Hitler rose from very obscure origins to become the supreme leader of Germany, and in the process, some 50 million people lost their lives in the most cataclysmic war to this time. Victims included 6 million Jews who were singled out, not because they opposed the dictator (you can expect any dictator to kill off the opposition), but simply because they were Jews. One of the most monstrous crimes in history was the loading of women, children, men, young and old, and whoever Hitler could get his hands on, into railroad cars, taking them to prison camps such as Treblinka and Auschwitz, and simply murdering them. (Many of the railroad cars had been taken from the German army, which desperately needed supplies on the eastern front.) This is how his legacy will be remembered. What people don't understand is the root problem at the base of Hitler's crimes, the same type of thinking seen so much of today in the New Age movement.

Why did Adolf Hitler commit these crimes? Recently, there was a full-page report in the Austin *American Statesman* on the Holocaust. They said that no one could understand what had happened, after all Adolf Hitler was a Christian. He had professed a belief in "positive Christianity." Was he a Christian, and if so, why did he commit these unspeakable acts?

Hitler being a Christian is absolutely untrue. Although he was born in the Catholic Church, he rejected catholicism at the age of 14 or 15, and he held the Protestant Church in even lower esteem. He could in no way be called a Christian, but he was not a man without a religion. Adolf Hitler was very religious, and it was those religious convictions that led to the Holocaust. Hitler's religion, which was very common, was founded out of what was called the "occult revival" in the late nineteenth century. Specifically, Hitler believed in the tenets of what is now known as theosophy. Various theosophical societies are alive today and are part of the New Age movement, but they all grew out of the same movement in the nineteenth century, most typified by Madame Blavatsky's Theosophical Society. There is no evidence that Hitler was ever a member of a theosophical society or any of its sub-units. But the kind of thinking that is represented by the doctrines of theosophy permeated most of Europe at that time to an extent not believed to be possible until you research the occult revival. It is those very doctrines that led Hitler to want to exterminate the Jews.

Hitler also believed that a shadowy hierarchy of ascended masters had chosen him as the vehicle to bring in a one-world order. He definitely considered himself the chosen one and claimed on many occasions to have direct communications with God Himself. The standard feature of the theosophical type of thinking that made up many of Hitler's opinions calls for a shadowy group of ascended masters that control the destiny of the world. Depending upon which theosophical source is used, there are either 7, 9, 63, or millions of ascended masters.

In the mid-1930s, 1,000 Tibetan monks were brought to Berlin by the SS and Heinrich Himmler, because they believed the Tibetan version of Buddhism was the earliest and most pure form of the ancient religions that are supposedly at the core of all religions. You and I know that there is an ancient religion at the core of all religions (except Christianity), and that's the ancient Babylonian religion. If you follow Hitler's religion, the New Age movement, and any number of the eccentric, non-Christian religions straight back to their source, you find they are all nothing but the old Babylonian mystery teachings updated for time and circumstance. They're Mystery Babylon updated, and this shouldn't come as a great surprise to any Christian who reads the Bible. Revelation 17 tells us that in the last days Mystery Babylon will be restored.

In discussing Hitler being the chosen one or chosen vehicle, in occult terminology he is like a "vessel" or "container." What goes into this "vessel" or "container"? What motivated him? Was he demon-possessed? He was not only demon-possessed, but also probably quite mad or insane. Most people don't realize that just because a person is demon-possessed and insane doesn't mean that person can't function as a head of state.

Many of Hitler's actions were fueled by his occultic religious beliefs. For example, no one can understand the Holocaust unless they understand the doctrines behind it. According to the New Age movement and Hitler's beliefs, today mankind is made up of seven root races, of which the fifth root race is the white Aryan, northern European man. According to Nazi doctrine, the earlier root races (of which the Jews are supposedly representative) are trying to keep these white Aryan, northern European people from jumping to the status of the sixth root race, which are supernatural, psychic individuals. The only way to make the jump is to cleanse or purify the race. Cleansing and purifying is something the Nazis had very much on their minds, and the whole idea was to get rid of everyone who was not of the same race. Even though the Nazis started with the Jews because of the particular hatred they had for them, the argument is very convincing that their real hatred was for Jesus Christ. However, they were not courageous enough to take on Jesus Christ, so instead of hating the Jews as the Christ-givers, they had to hate them as the Christ-killers. The Nazis invented their vile doctrine and went after the Jews first. But they weren't going to stop with the Jews. After World War II, it was discovered that they were going to eliminate the Jews and Gypsies first, then the Slavs (Polish and other Eastern Europeans), and eventually blacks and others would fall under the cleansing doctrine of the Nazis. They would then have a pure Aryan, superman race.

A seven-volume edition of the New Age bible attempts to interpret and pervert the Holy Bible in light of New Age doctrine. It discusses the seven root races and claims the highest to which man can attain, which used to be Aryan, is now Aquarian. The Aryan man can become the Aquarian man. Because this is the age of Aquarius, the Aquarian is the superman. The Aquarian man might is what Hitler had in mind when he talked about the superman. The superman is the same being, the sixth root race man that New Agers identify. Some call him *homouniversalis* or universal man, while others call him *homoknowaticus* or knowing man and by this last term they mean *knosis*, a Greek word that infers direct, experiential knowledge of God, as well as psychic powers and abilities. The modern New Agers see the homo-knowaticus in a very positive light, but even Adolf Hitler was afraid of the new man. He once remarked to Hermann Roschling (one of his followers who defected early in the Third Reich and formed one of the most reliable sources for Hitler's early occultism),

"I have seen the superman, and he frightens me."

Those who believe this is going to be a great transition ought to listen to Hitler. If he was afraid of the new man, perhaps everyone should be. A document about one of the organizations that teaches the homouniversalis doctrine states that they are addressing a world in which only 500 million people live. This means that they must kill 5.5 billion people to achieve this nice New Age world.

In Elberton, Georgia, a group of stones are put together much like Stonehenge in the Keltic (Celtic) Druid area of Great Britain. Similar sites have also been found in Texas, New Hampshire, and Wisconsin, and each site is supposed to be a conjunction of one of the earth's currents. They are also supposedly energy points. There is a story about the site in Georgia. A stranger came to town, offered to erect the stone site, and persuaded the city officials to agree. He erected this New Age monument and on it is inscribed the homouniversalis belief of a 500 million-person planet. The only way to do that is starve, disease, or murder 5.5 billion people.

Hitler was a mad man, but mad men can use and act upon occult religious beliefs in a very rational, logical way, with premeditation. This is also true of serial killers and mass murderers throughout history. They don't kill at random, they have a scheme or design, a plan. Many don't realize that Hitler and others were thinking very logically. What people don't understand is their frame of reference. We think from our frame of reference, which is based on Christian values, so we are unable to even conceive of these crimes. What happens is that mad or insane individuals adopt a different frame of reference. In the case of Hitler, it was what we would call today a New Age frame of reference. Suddenly, the murder of millions becomes reasonable. After all, aren't you doing good by cleansing the race so that man can jump to a better, higher state? That may seem incredible to us, but it doesn't seem incredible for someone whose world view would make that the logical thing to do.

Obviously, if you are a fundamental, evangelical Christian, you will not be happy in a New Age world.

All you have to do is turn on the TV, and the sin and debauchery will simply upset you and make you angry. Slasher movies such as *Nightmare on Elm Street* are also likely to be upsetting. Even when you read the newspaper, your conscience will torture you. There is a way out of all of this so your negative thought processes will not harm the earth. Wouldn't it be better to put you out of your misery, and then in your next life you might return as a New Ager. You never really die, you're born-again.

Many men in the SS were taught that they weren't actually harming their Jewish victims in an ultimate sense. They might return as Aryans in their next life; this was one way in which they salved their conscience. Those in the SS did have consciences, which was a major problem for the killing crews. You cannot persuade men to kill others and not have it affect them personally. This helped to salve their consciences and obtain a few more weeks of killing from them by claiming they were ultimately helping the Jews by relieving them of the burdens of this life as a lower form of man, and perhaps they would come back as Aryans next time. The reincarnation belief is extremely horrible when you consider that many people will fail to help those in need because they might interfere with the process of reincarnation and the working off of bad karma. The only reason there were righteous Gentiles in Europe to save some of the Jews is that the Eastern religious views of karma and reincarnation were not as widespread as in the East. What would have happened if this had occurred in Central or Southeast Asia? If this had happened in an area with people for whom helping somebody being carried off to a gas chamber would be interfering with their pre-chosen karma, would there have been any righteous Gentiles?

What would happen if someone like Hitler rose to power in the United States? Today in this country, there are 35 to 50 million people who believe in various forms of New Ageism. According to one recent poll, 23 percent of Americans believe in reincarnation. What would prevent these kinds of crimes from occurring here since the moral base and fiber of this nation has been shattered? The answer is nothing. Germany was considered to have attained the heighth of human achievement in the arts and sciences to that time. When the mind of man pushed back the frontiers of knowledge at the end of the nineteenth century, that mind mostly thought in German, so much so that science and engineering students were once required to learn German. Germany was at the highest pinnacle of civilization. Yet because of the liberal higher criticism that devastated the German church in the late nineteenth century, there were no moral underpinnings. Basically, they had built their house on a foundation of sand. What happened when the storm came? The sand washed away and the foundation crumbled. We may be very smug in thinking that none of these things can ever happen here, but if it happened in Germany, it can happen in the United States.

Is it possible that another Adolf Hitler could rise to power in the 1990s? Events are occurring in Europe today; could they culminate in an Antichrist, a horrible son of perdition, the man of sin (2 Thess. 2:3)? Jesus said, *"And when these things begin to come to pass, then look up . . . for your redemption draweth nigh"* (Luke 21:28). We are cautioned against setting dates and times, however Scripture encourages us to look for the signs of the times (Matt. 16:3) because that's how we'll know when the end is near.

Peter stated very clearly in 2 Peter 3:3-4, *"Knowing this first, that there shall come in the last days scoffers, walking after their own lusts, And saying, Where is the promise of his coming? for since the fathers fell asleep, all things continue as they were. . . ."* Isn't that true today? One example is what is happening now in Europe. Those in the New Age and occult movements say, "It could never happen again. After all, history books tells us about Hitler. It will never happen again." To those in the pulpit who believe this, get out of the pulpit because you don't belong there. To others, simply look around. People will tell you that you can prove anything with Scripture, but that isn't the case. If you apply the ordinary rules of scriptural interpretation, you come up with a standard scenario of what will happen. You can't force fit too many other scenarios into those rules. What is happening today looks almost like it fits, looks like a very close fit. While avoiding setting a date, its time to look up and make sure we keep our eyes on Jesus.

Previously, we discussed the 50 million people, including 6 million Jews, killed during World War II, the death camps, Hitler's race theories based on the occult, New Age doctrine, and the cleansing of the earth. The idea for the title of *The Twisted Cross* by Joseph Carr came from a statement in one of the major, national news magazines. (The article was about fundamentalist Christians, so it didn't really apply.) The article stated,

"With enough distortion, a cross will become a swastika."

In thinking about this, central Europe had been very Christianized at the beginning of the nineteenth century, but by 1920 when Hitler began to become politically active and started his ascent to power, what had been taught as good doctrine had become distorted so badly that many who had been nominally raised in the church were able to be influenced by Hitler's ideas. Those ideas were of Hindu origin, as is the swastika. These people had distorted their doctrine to the point where they could accept these New Age ideas and build an entire government from them.

The swastika is commonly found in Hindu

temples in India. In the film *Gods of the New Age* by Pat and Caryl Matrisciana, one of the scenes includes temples in India adorned with swastikas that are still there even today. Temples in Japan have swastikas, and native American Indians also used them. This goes back to the Mystery Babylon religion, the worship of the sun god. The swastika is a form of a twisted cross, but it's also the sun rays used by those involved in the worship of the sun god. It's a symbol used by many Eastern religions, and it's found on every continent except the islands of the Pacific and Australia. Virtually everywhere else, that symbol is common among the ancient indigenous cultures. The swastika is literally a worldwide symbol with Satan at its roots.

Yet today people say that there must have been something very peculiar about the Germans. Of course, we Americans would never do what they did. The French are lovers, they would never do anything like the Germans did. The British would never do anything so horrible as genocide. How can we answer the various ethnic groups that say, "Oh no, that was the Germans"?

Look at the German SS and the kind of people who made up the SS. Some contend they were thugs or congenital malcontents that would have been in trouble in any society in which they were members. However, the truth is quite different. The SS were an elite military group; they were drawn from the cream of the crop. The men who joined the SS, including perhaps many of those involved in the horrible crimes the SS committed, were from phenomenally middle-class, Roman Catholic, Lutheran, and evangelical families. These are good credentials. These were the sons of shopkeepers, judges, physicians. These were not the congenital thugs who would have been criminals in any society, they were the best Germany had to offer. In a country where less than 5 percent of the people went to church, we can't call Germany a Christian country in the sense we understand in the United States. But in a nation with nominal Christian values, Christian at least to the outside world, those who were members of the SS were transformed into brutal killers who were capable of committing almost any crime you can imagine. They were not very different from you and I. What is so awful about them is that before they were brainwashed and indoctrinated, these men were completely normal.

Could there be a revival of the SS in the world today? Although there is not a revival of the SS yet, there has been a continuation of the group. After World War II, virtually every SS member that could be found was arrested. Any soldier caught with an SS uniform was arrested and thrown into special camps until the four military powers that conquered Germany could sort everything out. For many years up to the early 1950s, first the Allies and then the Germans themselves conducted de-Nazification trials to discover which SS men were guilty of crimes and which were not.

However, within weeks after the end of World War II, the SS had reformed into clandestine underground cells. The famous Odessa group, a terrorist group, was mostly suppressed. One group formed into a veteran's organization, not unlike the Veterans of Foreign Wars and American Legion in our country, but they're only old soldiers getting together for a few drinking bouts. There were two major secret SS groups. One headed by Otto Skorzeny, the SS commando who rescued Mussolini and was quite a hero to the Germans, was called The Spider. This group apparently had access to a large amount of the SS treasury that had been deposited in banks, much of it stolen from concentration camp victims. They operated into the 1970s, and may well still be operating today. During the Battle of the Bulge, captured American troops were executed by the SS. The man who perpetrated this was released from jail in 1956 because, although he had been sentenced to death, this group was still able to influence the German government with their underground activities. The SS is definitely intact, and every once in a while, you hear of another German official who is disgraced by having his SS past revealed.

The evidence is overwhelming that many members of the SS not only survived the war, but entered the governments of both East and West Germany. After all, what happens when a society collapses, and you try to rebuild it? The American military wasn't going to run the country forever. Guess who were the people that already had the experience to run the police, the water works, the government bureaus? Who do you think they were? They were the men who served the Nazis, many of them SS. In order to make the society work, the governments of the United States, France, Great Britain, and the Soviet Union recruited many of the SS veterans and put them in positions of authority.

Recently, the world saw the fall of the Berlin Wall. Helmut Kohl went to Berlin to speak to a combined crowd of East and West Berliners. As he presented his speech and started to discuss reunification of East and West Germany, a determined number of people (not the majority) began to cry out, "We want a fourth reich!" Hitler talked about his Third Reich which he claimed would last for a thousand years. It is possible that the sentiment for a fourth reich combined with the events happening in Europe now could eventually culminate in a fourth reich. Everything that is now occurring in Eastern Europe is very interesting, but it is also a little disquieting. Some are saying this is the first female-style revolution in history. Nobody was killed, and everybody went shopping. But behind the news, there is a story that went unnoticed concerning those in East Germany traveling to West Berlin and going shopping. Neo-Nazis held rallies in Leipzig, indicating a strong and organized movement. Hopefully, if Germany is reunited, they will join the family of nations as a responsible member. But the facts are that twice in this century there have been problems with Germany and there is still neo-Nazi sentiment there, even though it is only a minority at this time. However, the Nazi party in 1919 had only 55 members. This is a situation which bears much scrutiny.

Many Europeans are worried about all of this, and want a United States of Europe. Rather than having a reunited German juggernaut with Germany controlling the continent, some Europeans propose a United States of Europe in which Germany would fit in with the entire nation/state, making it not as powerful. It is possible that Germany could give up hegemony to the other nations, although some of the nations are beginning to balk at the loss of sovereignty, a single European monetary system, and a stronger European parliament this would involve. One neck of a unified Germany only requires one leash. Hitler tried to conquer all of Europe. If all of Europe were united, it would be easy to simply take over the European government. If Hitler were alive today, this would accomplish all of his goals without having to resort to large wars. Hitler could impose a totalitarian government on all of the countries in Europe simply by getting a majority vote in the European parliament. Of all the European countries, the greatest force of all would be a united Germany, and they could dominate all of Europe. Then would come the fulfillment of Revelation 17, the revival in the last days of the great Roman Empire/Mystery Babylon international confederation where the beast will come to the fore. This would be frightening, unless from Bible prophecy we know how it's going to end. There will be some shocked people.

Most people feel that Gorbachev and what he is doing are wonderful, and that we're going to have world peace. However, until they begin destroying their arms and moving their military divisions away from the East-West lines, the capability to advance on Europe is still there. Let's assume in the absolute best case that Gorbachev is what he seems to be and the changes in Eastern Europe are real. What makes everyone think these changes are for the better? Eastern Europe is not exactly overrun with Jeffersonian democrats who understand the concepts of the rights of man and the government deriving authority from the consent of the people, the kinds of things we cherish here in the United States. Who can say that the next group who takes over won't be just as bad as the previous group? Just as Nazis were taken into the German government after World War II because the new government needed an infrastructure, at the end of the day when all the revolutionaries have stopped shopping and have returned to their houses and their jobs, the buses still have to run, the waterworks still have to churn out water, electricity still has to be generated. Guess who the people are that know how to run Eastern Europe? The communists who were supposedly just removed from power. After all the free elections have been completed, Eastern Europe may still have communist governments in power. Lech Walesa is probably a national hero and a great man, but how much does a shipyard electrician know about running a national economy or national government? He will have to depend a lot on the bureaucrats who have been there the last 40 years, and they aren't democrats and republicans.

There is something called the Revolution of Rising Expectations. When people's hopes are aroused and then their expectations are not met, they can become quite furious. Historian Crane Britain once wrote a book on that subject, and he pointed out that revolutions do not generally succeed or even occur with a totally suppressed people. In every case of major revolutions in the last 300 years, the expectations of the people in their condition didn't improve quickly enough. The Soviet Union is sitting on a powder keg. When things became restless enough that it appeared there might be a revolution, the classic answer for a totalitarian government whose people are about to revolt is to engage in a foreign military adventure. The next thing we know there could be war.

There is another solution when people become desperate, and many are becoming very desperate. Eastern Europeans have overthrown the Romanian dictator, and have also overthrown communists in other countries. In Russia, Lithuania, Armenia, and Azerbaidzhan are working hard to overthrow the Communist Party in their regions. Even if they are able to do that, men such as Vaclav Havel in Czechoslovakia and Lech Walesa in Poland don't have the ability to give their countries the material goods they're demanding. Revelation 6:2 says, *"And I saw, and behold a white horse: and he that sat on him had a bow; and a crown was given unto him: and he went forth conquering, and to conquer."* Because of the desperation and economic chaos that surrounds Eastern Europe, could the people of those countries seek the man on the white horse? Those in desperate straits always reach out for whatever man on a white horse or miraculous situation will pull them out of their problems. Oddly enough, there is one Savior people never seem to look for, and He is Jesus Christ.

Revelation has two riders on white horses. Revelation 6 tells about the four horsemen of the apocalypse, and verse 8 says, *"And I looked, and behold a pale horse: and his name that sat on him was Death, and Hell followed with him. And power was given unto them over the fourth part of the earth, to kill with sword, and with hunger, and with death. . . ."* At the end of the story, Revelation 19 describes another rider on a white horse, totally different from those before, Jesus Christ, King of kings and Lord of lords, and He will bring in His millennial kingdom.

Adolf Hitler also spoke of a 1,000-year millennial reign by the Nazis, a 1,000-year reich which only lasted 12 years, a counterfeit. It is interesting that Jesus promises to return with man at the end of all things here on earth and bring in a 1,000-year millennium. Hitler was very fond of comparing himself with Jesus Christ. He said,

"Jesus Christ failed, whereas I became chancellor."

But the Bible says that Jesus came to destroy the works of the devil, and He did so on the cross. Christians have this great promise.

Chapter Three
A Revived Holy Roman Empire?

by J.R. Church

This chapter continues with what Bible prophecy reveals concerning the future United States of Europe. Several years ago, if this ministry had presented programs on this subject, people would have literally laughed. "What do you mean Europe is rising? What is a United States of Europe?" But incredible events have taken place in 1989 and continue to occur in 1990. The Berlin Wall has come down. What is happening behind the Iron Curtain? What do the events occurring in Romania, Czechoslovakia, Hungary, Poland, and East Germany mean? Do these things presage a revival of the Holy Roman Empire? What does Bible prophecy say? What does this signify for your life and those of your loved ones? The only thing we can be sure of is that everything God said would transpire will occur.

There are many things we can't take a chance on today. When you drive your car, most of the time the brakes work, but there might be one time in which they don't. Most of the time, airplanes will fly you to your destination, but every once in a while they don't. These are man-made things. God's Word is God-made. Through Bible prophecy it is possible to discover what these events in Europe portend. Do these events foreshadow a revived Holy Roman Empire?

Many evangelists and teachers quote from *Prophecy in the News* by J.R. Church. In the January 1990 edition, one of the headlines was, "Leaders Forging a New World Order" written by Gary Stearman. The article says:

> *"The Bush-Gorbachev summit couldn't have been better described than it was in a front page article in the* New York Times. *'From Malta, President Bush and President Mikhail Gorbachev of the Soviet Union arrived today for a summit conference, during which both hope to start the search for a new world order.' "*

The *New York Times* used the very words considered by many to be the conspiratorial theory of "a new world order." One of the main themes of Bible prophecy is that there will one day be a so-called new world order established by an Antichrist system of government to try to eliminate God from the human race. It is amazing that they were so blatant to actually use the term. They are not, as the article states, beginning to forge a new world order; they've been working toward this end for a very long time. It's only now becoming visible to the general public. For those who have been watching this for years, we know that this has been happening.

The new world order is spoken of throughout the entire Bible. The prophet Daniel was given a vision of four great world empires, typified as beasts. *"Thus he said, The fourth beast shall be the fourth kingdom upon earth, which shall be diverse from all kingdoms, and shall devour the whole earth, and shall tread it down, and break it in pieces. And the ten horns out of this kingdom are ten kings that shall arise . . ."* (Dan. 7:23-24). Can we see the beginnings of the fourth beast empire today?

The fourth beast actually began with the rise of the original Roman Empire. Although it crumbled, over the centuries it has sputtered along as European monarchs have tried to revive it from time to time. To use a metaphor, Humpty Dumpty has had a great fall, and curiously it is the king's men who are trying to put Humpty Dumpty back together again, not the butcher, the baker, or the candlestick maker. It is not the average man on the street but the politicians who have been trying to reunify the Roman Empire, and they will succeed, although for only a short time.

What is the connection between the ancient Roman Empire and the modern-day European situation? The politicians in Europe today, the movers and shakers of European politics, are actually from royal families which can be traced through the monarchies of Europe all the way back to the Roman Empire.

There has been infighting between relatives through the centuries with European wars being fought to try to capture territories. The demise of the final remnants of the Roman Empire in 1806 along with the renaissance in Europe throughout the 1800s saw the toppling of many European thrones. When Charles I, deposed king of Austria, was exiled for life following World War I, the monarchies of Europe finally realized that they must work together to restore European dominance. European monarchs lost everything their ancestors had worked toward for the past 1,500 years. In 1921, the Pan-European movement began with mainly the royal families and monarchies deciding they must reunite Europe. Then Hitler rose to power and struck another blow to their plans.

Some feel that monarchs have no importance in today's world, yet they are fascinated by Prince Charles and Princess Diana of Great Britain, and Queen Julianna of the Netherlands. Is there a renaissance of the monarchs, something happening behind the scenes that most people don't understand? Beneath the glitter of the royalty, is something economic or political developing of which we should be aware?

Adolf Hitler was a wicked and evil man, an antichrist if there ever was one. When he struck another blow to the plans of the European monarchs, it did not necessarily mean that was a good thing. The relationship between Hitler and other conspirators in Europe was like mafia infighting where one criminal fights another for territorial control. Hitler didn't care about the Aryan race; it is obvious that his bid for power was personal. He wanted to be in control. Historically, Hitler had an obscure background and although no one is sure of his heritage, there is speculation that he actually rose from European royalty. Hitler's father was illegitimate, and no one knows who Hitler's grandfather was. It is thought by many in Europe that Hitler's father was an illegitimate son of someone in the German monarchy. If this is true, it would help to explain how he was able to rise so quickly to power and dismantle the union that Otto von Habsburg and others were trying to achieve through the Pan-European movement.

Otto von Habsburg had to flee to the United States during World War I, and it was during his stay in America that he convinced President Rossevelt to allow him to try to establish an army of Austrians near Washington, D.C. so he could return to Austria with this army and regain his throne. He tried desperately to enlist an army for Habsburg to invade Austria during World War II, but the attempt failed. Immediately after the war, Habsburg returned to Europe and began to try to arouse interest in forming a United States of Europe.

Concerning research on the development of the Common Market, there are significant dates in its formation that coincide with the dates of the formation of the nation of Israel. This is not just a coincidence.

In 1948, the coal and steel industry of six European nations combined to start a cooperation of economic unity which is almost the year the state of Israel officially became a nation. In 1949, the Council of Europe began to work toward a common economic recovery for all of Europe. The recovery centered in Germany which experienced a post-war economic miracle. Many of us remember how Volkswagens flooded the United States during the 1950s and 1960s. The next significant date is 1957 when the Common Market was formed with Belgium, France, Italy, Luxembourg, the Netherlands, and West Germany. Those six nations had already formed alliances through their coal and steel industries, and in 1957 the Atomic Energy Commission of Europe was also brought in which greatly enhanced their image throughout Europe as a unified group. As the years progressed, the Common Market and the European Economic Community became integrated as one body.

On August 9, 1949, Israel ended its first great war with the Arabs, which is the same year the Council of Europe began. Israel's second war was in 1956-1957, the same year the Common Market organized officially as a group, and the third was in 1967, the Six-Day War. The Common Market became the European Economic Community in 1967. This may look like a coincidence to many, but in God's plan there is no coincidence. What has and is happening in modern-day Israel since 1948 directly corresponds to the unification of Europe. Key events in the history of these two political, economic entities are occurring simultaneously. Only God could design this and cause events to occur.

What was the next momentous date in Israel's history after 1967? It was 1973 and the Yom Kippur War, and also that year Denmark, Ireland, and Great Britain joined the EEC, bringing its membership to nine nations. Shortly thereafter, Greece became the tenth nation in the EEC and was followed by Spain and Portugal. In 1979, at about the time of the next series of developments in the life of Israel, came the EEC coinage, the first discussions of a common European currency, a unit called the ecu. The history of Israel seems to parallel the history of the European Common Market.

If the historical events in the life of modern-day Israel have paralleled what is happening in Europe in the formation of a new Holy Roman Empire, then what about the last days event in which the Antichrist will make a covenant with Israel? Is the world being propelled to that remarkable event in history? The fulfillment of Bible prophecy revolves around the re-establishment of the nation of Israel. The Bible perceives everything from a Middle Eastern perspective, not a European perspective. Nations mentioned in prophecy are all nations that have a relation with Israel. Throughout the prophecies of Scripture, everything is seen from an Israeli point of view because the prophets who wrote them were Jewish. God gave the message to the Jewish prophets for one reason: although God was going to disperse the Jews among the nations of the world, it was also God who was going to gather the Jews back to their promised land for the last seven years before the Messiah would come to save them and set up the kingdom. When the kingdom is established for 1,000 years, it will be a kingdom ruled from Jerusalem — not Moscow, London, Paris, Rome, Washington, or Tokyo, but Jerusalem. It will be a Jewish world kingdom. This may be difficult for Gentiles to accept, but this is what will happen according to Bible prophecy. After all, Jesus Christ is the Messiah, and He is a Jew.

Christians who deny that God has a predestined role for Israel miss all the fantastic events that are happening now. How can you fully understand the mysteries and wonders of God unless you accept the role for Israel that God has prophesied for them in His Word?

When you read the prophecies in the Old Testament and God's promises to Abraham, Isaac, Jacob, Jacob's twelve sons, the tribe of Judah, and the house of David, you must realize that if God doesn't keep His promises to them, He may not keep his promises to us. God said in Psalm 89:35, *"Once have I sworn by my holiness that I will not lie unto David."* God is not a liar, so when God says He has a covenant with the chosen people, the twelve tribes of Israel, we should accept it. Revelation clearly says there will be 12,000 from each tribe of Israel. God has everything worked out mathematically, and the historical sequence of events proves the majesty of God.

Revelation 17 discusses the last-days world system with ten kings. *"These have one mind, and shall give their power and strength unto the beast"* (Rev. 17:13). However, verse 17 says that it is God's will that they do so. They have no option. Some people may be frightened because of all that is happening at this time in history and what is to come in the future. Should they be? People should look to Jesus because He has everything in control. He's the monarch who is coming to rule, and His monarchy will be a theocracy. It will be the golden age, the utopia, that man has dreamed for down through the centuries. Only Satan will be fighting against it, and most of us would rather be on the winning side. The peace that passes all understanding in Christ Jesus comes from the knowledge that He controls the clock. He has all the events scheduled, they are all in His control. All we have to do is watch. Look up, because Jesus is coming again!

Chapter Four

King of Jerusalem

by J.R. Church

The world situation today will startle, shock, and even frighten you if you don't know Jesus Christ. If you know the Lord, the study of Bible prophecy will only strengthen your faith. God said that what is happening now would occur as part of His majestic and mighty plan.

In the previous chapter, a passage from Daniel was quoted mentioning the fourth kingdom of the beast, the last earthly kingdom. Is this fourth kingdom coming in the future, or is it already here? The reunification of Europe is slated to arrive in 1992, called the United States of Europe. Europe has been moving toward this unity for many years. This is no accident of history, not an aberration or afterthought.

For centuries, many have tried to reunite the Roman Empire. Throughout history, one European monarch after another would start a war with another nation, usually ruled by a relative, and try to gain territory by capturing other countries to establish a united states of Europe, but none succeeded. Napoleon tried and even abolished the throne of the Holy Roman Empire in order to empower himself as the

41

leader of a new Europe and eventually a world government. He even married the daughter of the deposed Habsburg emperor of the Holy Roman Empire to sire a son whom he called "the king of Rome." Napoleon planned to work toward fulfilling his dream of his son becoming the world ruler.

Descendants of the Habsburgs are alive today. What role does the Habsburg dynasty presently play in the coming United States of Europe, and how does all of this correspond with Bible prophecy? The Habsburg dynasty can be traced to Merovig in the fifth century A.D. who lent his name to the dynasty known as the Merovingian dynasty. During medieval Europe, legend of the Holy Grail grew around the Habsburgs, and they claimed to be the family of the Holy Grail, which gave them a divine right to rule not only Europe, but the entire world. For over 500 years, the Habsburgs provided the emperors of the Holy Roman Empire, from 1271 A.D. when Rudolph I became the first Habsburg emperor until 1806 when Napoleon abolished the throne. However, Napoleon married a Habsburg, Marie Louise, because he wanted to keep the bloodline alive, knowing that the family of the Holy Grail would eventually become rulers of the entire world. (The Holy Grail is an esoteric, Mystery Babylon-type religion.) Napoleon's dream was a world government. Even though the formation of a revived Roman Empire was effectively abolished in 1806 with the French Revolution, the rise of Napoleon, and the renaissance of the 1800s, everyone still looked to the Habsburgs for leadership and guidance. When Francis Ferdinand Habsburg was assassinated in 1914 precipitating World War I, it opened the door for the Habsburgs to try to redevelop the idea of a United States of Europe.

Today, the Habsburgs still hold the title, King of Jerusalem, established by Godfrey de Bouillon when he captured Jerusalem in 1099 A.D. and founded a Crusader kingdom. The goal of the Crusades was to bring Jerusalem under control of the Christians. But what the Habsburg dynasty was trying to accomplish through the Crusades was to institute the millennial kingdom and the throne of David. They were going to be the God-ordained rulers of the millennium, similar to the Dominion Theology of today in which the aim is to bring in the kingdom without the real King, Jesus Christ. All of this relates to a conspiracy to bring in a one-world order, a kingdom of men led by Satan, rather than the biblical prescription that Jesus Christ will reign in the millennial kingdom.

The March 20, 1989 edition of *U.S. News and World Report*, which is not known as a journal of biblical prophecy, contains a headline which reads, "President Habsburg?"

"Are the Habsburgs headed for a comeback in Hungary? As preposterous as the notion may sound, communist officials in Budapest are

floating the idea that Otto von Habsburg, eldest son of the last emperor of the Austrian-Hungarian monarchy and now a member of the European parliament representing Bavaria, could be asked to become the ceremonial chief of state under the new constitution scheduled to go in to effect next year."

The latest events in Eastern Europe could mean that Habsburg may have great influence.

Otto von Habsburg is 67 years old and was the key man in the composition of the 1948 European Economic Community, originally called the Council of Europe (1948-1949). In 1951, the European Coal and Steel Community was organized to unify the coal, iron, and steel industries. Habsburg was the man behind the scenes putting all of this together. As he traveled in Europe, he was able to convince Belgium, France, Italy, Luxembourg, the Netherlands, and West Germany to form a coalition of nations in 1957 called the European Economic Community. (The term "Common Market" did not appear until 1967.) Habsburg was one of the principals behind this European union. Today, being one of the leading delegates of the European parliament, he is still working toward the day when Europe will become a united state in 1992.

When Hungary ousted the communists a few months ago, they immediately scheduled elections for

November and invited Habsburg to run for president, but he declined. He probably would have won very easily, so why did he demur? Otto von Habsburg does not want to be simply the monarch of a little country, he wants a larger role in European affairs. In 1992 as the thirteenth nation joins the European United States, Habsburg will be ready for a major role in what will eventually become a one-world government and economy.

We are not naming the Antichrist, but certain events and certain people, Habsburg being one of them, are being propelled by God's will into the center stage of world affairs. At this moment, Satan is lord of this world. Habsburg and others simply have a key role in what appears to be the future one-world government. To repeat, we're not saying that a Habsburg is the Antichrist, although God may reveal who the Antichrist is through future events. But if we refrain from mentioning Otto von Habsburg and his role in the European Common Market, we would be leaving out one of the most important elements of not only Bible prophecy, but also the developing United States of Europe. The history of man, the history of the Roman Empire, and the development of modern-day Europe revolves around this man and his ancestors.

An article in the *London Sunday Telegraph*, November 26, 1989, relates how other Habsburg descendants are waiting in the background to take their turn on the world stage. The article, "Habsburg's

Hopefuls Hover in the Wings," reports on the funeral of Empress Zita, the mother of Otto von Habsburg, who died in March 1989. She was memorialized by 50,000 people attending a large funeral in Vienna. Later, another memorial service was held in England which the *London Sunday Telegraph* covered. The article reveals the feelings in Europe about the monarchies that are resurging at this time.

> *"Father Charles Roux, who conducted the service . . . compared her fate, and that of her husband, to Marie-Antoinette and Louis XVI. 'The history of the dynasty was put on parade, but the future was not forgotten.' At the European parliament six weeks ago — I forget how long, but it was in the* Financial Times, *a long article — who was it who proposed the re-establishment of the Holy Roman Empire? It was Otto, Otto von Habsburg, and another Otto, Otto von Bismarck.' Father Charles Roux spoke for nearly an half an hour about the marvels of the Holy Roman Empire."*

This was before an audience of European nobles gathered from all over Europe to memorialize the Empress Zita. It was almost spine-chilling as the Austrian national anthem was played at the end of the service and tears flowed from every eye.

When the statement is made that Otto von Habsburg was the brains behind the developing

United States of Europe, this is not something considered to be only a possibility. An article in the *London Sunday Telegraph* says absolutely that he was. Otto von Habsburg is the man who has put everything together. His son, Karl, is following in his father's footsteps. Karl is in his late twenties, so by the year 2000 A.D., he'll be in his late thirties, a very productive and energetic time in his life, ready to assume leadership in Europe. Karl is also a very handsome young man. Again, this is not to say that he is going to be an antichrist or anything remotely similar. But the Antichrist will be a dazzling figure on the world scene, a charmer. One thing is certain: the Bible says at a certain time during the tribulation period, the Antichrist will go to Jerusalem and usurp the throne of David, claiming title to King of Jerusalem. Otto von Habsburg holds that title today, and his son, Karl, is heir to the title. It is only a titular title; there is no throne in Jerusalem, yet.

Today, Europe is experiencing a resurgence of love for the monarchy, with interest in it spreading worldwide to Australia, New Zealand, Canada, and even here in the United States. Two magazines now found in the United States completely devote all their issues to reports on European royalty. People are fantasizing what the world would be like if Prince Charming were to rule the earth. In a coming issue of *Bible in the News*, the question is asked, "Is Prince Charles a New Ager?" The answer comes from a major New Age magazine from Australia, *Odyssey*, which praises Prince Charles very highly. The article discusses his role in the world environmental movement and New Age movement. It is very shocking but the documentation comes from New Agers themselves. Once again, the monarchy is involved in New Age affairs.

The family of the Holy Grail is actually the underlying foundation of the New Age movement. The legend of the Holy Grail is a New Age concept. The New Age movement is not new, it is old European, medieval witchcraft involving the Holy Grail. The Holy Grail was considered to be many things, not just a cup that Jesus held. The Holy Grail is a crystal ball used in the medieval seance rooms. It is also a stone of light, the philosopher's stone, the capstone on top of a pyramid, or the pineal gland at the base of the brain. It's also the all-seeing eye. Many are saying today that they are on a quest for the Holy Grail. What does this mean? It is the descent of the sun god into the human body, the worship of the sun, moon, and stars to become gods. This is the idolatry of the Old Testament and has been going on almost since time began. According to Revelation 17, this type of worship will be restored in the last days and is pictured as Mystery Babylon. The last-days worldwide church of Satan will be this Babylonian system which is the quest for the Holy Grail, the quest for the Babylonian practices, traditions, and rituals, which is witchcraft.

Some years ago, a European statesman made a statement to the delegates of the United Nations,

"Give us a man who can solve the problems of Europe, and we will follow him. We will follow him, even if it be the devil himself."

What a declaration!

The dark side of the appeal of the monarchy is anti-Semitism. The Jews went through a terrible Holocaust which reached its peak in 1944, but helped to encourage many Jews to return to their promised land. However, anti-Semitism is once again on the rise. One example is an article in the *New York Times* by Mr. P. Allmark, former deputy prime minister in Sweden and now a contributing editor to the *New York Times*. The article is about Radio Islam, similar to a clear channel station here in the United States, which runs 24 hours a day in Europe broadcasting anti-Semitic programming. They talk about how there is a Jewish conspiracy to rule the world, how Judaism has an evil nature, and how it will weaken and ravage the world. The following is an example of what is broadcast:

"Judaism, the Torah, and the Talmud stink of racism and contempt for other people."

Mr. Allmark says this garbage is spewing out of

Radio Islam continually, and he is amazed that no one is objecting. He asks where is our conscience?

We live in a generation that seems to have forgotten the lessons of history. This study has brought history back from the Roman Empire through the days of the Merovingians, Napoleon, Hitler, and to today. This history has great significance for today. God said all of this would happen in the end times as Satan would be kicked out of Heaven and come down to the earth having great wrath, knowing he has only a short time (Rev. 12:12). He will institute one of the most devastating periods of world history, and unless Jesus returns to save the world, *". . . there should no flesh be saved. . ."* (Matt. 24:22). The Antichrist must arise to power, there must be a battle involving Gog and Magog, and there must be a mark of the beast. All these things must come to pass. The Bible says they are like birth pangs in the birth of a new golden age. The next millennium, the seventh 1,000-year period of human history, should be the Great Sabbath, in which Jesus will reign as King of kings and Lord of lords. He is alive , and He is coming.

Chapter Five

Money — The Root of Europe's Problem

by J.R. Church

God's Word states that certain events would occur in the last days, and those events are transpiring today. A recent tabloid carried the headline, "Psychics Predict 1990." A study reports that their 1989 predictions were only 20 percent accurate. That's not good enough for God and His prophecies. A Christian television program had a guest who said he was beginning a prophet school to train prophets of Christianity. When the prophets first come, they are only 50 percent accurate, but with proper training, a Christian prophet can work up to a 90 percent accuracy rate. Is this something to be proud of? The Lord says in Isaiah, *"Remember the former things of old: for I am God, and there is none else. . . . Declaring the end from the beginning, and from ancient times the things that are not yet done, saying, My counsel shall stand . . ."* (Isa. 46:9-10). When God says something, He is 100 percent correct. None of us can claim to be prophets because any of us could be wrong in our summations. All anyone involved with this ministry can do is try to come as close as possible to what is happening at the present time in relation to biblical prophecy.

When the communist governments of Eastern Europe began to fall apart, and the Russian Revolution began to lose its grip upon its slaves, many theologians had to rethink what they had said previously about the world situation. Many asked what was happening, how did this relate to Ezekiel 38 and 39, the battle of Gog and Magog? Jesus told His disciples they wouldn't understand prophecy until after the prophecy was fulfilled. That's the problem theologians face today, especially fortune-tellers and Jean Dixon-type prognosticators. Most believe there are no more biblical prophets today, only students of prophecy. The Bible is complete, and there are no more new revelations.

In seeing biblical prophecies fulfilled with 100 percent accuracy, we should refer to Deuteronomy where we are told specifically that if just one prophecy from a prophet does not come to pass, then that person is not of God. But when we turn to the Bible, the prophecies from God's prophets all come to pass.

In considering Europe and what is happening in the communist bloc, there is a possibility that the fourth kingdom from Daniel is materializing at this time. The fourth beast of Daniel 7 was the Roman Empire of 2,000 years ago, but the ten horns that arose upon that head is the attempt to revive that beast in the last days. The dream of Nebuchadnezzar described a large man with a head of gold, which was the Babylonian Empire; the arms of silver represented the Medo-Persian Empire; the midsection of brass represented the Grecian Empire; and the two legs of iron represented the divided Roman Empire. Eventually, the image ends with the clay and iron in the ten toes of the beast, and this is what is developing in Europe today. That the Bible describes an image of ten toes doesn't mean that the revived Roman Empire will be comprised of only ten nations. The European Economic Community already has 12 members. Turkey was recently rejected for membership, but Austria is now bidding to become the thirteenth member. Future additions could include Hungary, Romania, Poland, and other Warsaw Pact nations if they are given enough time.

Also, at some time in the future, the battle of Gog and Magog will begin, and the Warsaw Pact nations of Gomer and Togarmah will ally with the Soviet Union. If this does not take place soon, unless the Soviet Union again invades the Eastern European countries attempting to change from communist to democratic governments, things may develop so that the battle of Gog and Magog will no longer be possible. The Soviet Union is falling apart very rapidly, and as students of Bible prophecy, we should be aware *"For when they shall say, Peace and safety; then sudden destruction cometh upon them . . ."* (1 Thess. 5:3). It is probable in the prophetic timetable

that the battle of Gog and Magog has been moved up.
It is not very likely that it could occur five years from
now. One or two years from now is more of a
possibility.

Gorbachev is pictured in the world media as a
beneficient, charismatic, wonderful leader who will
lead the world to a new era of economic peace, unity,
and strength. It's almost impossible to describe how
wonderful things will be when Gorbachev gets through
with *glasnost* and *perestroika*. In the economic sphere,
there is something known as "guns versus butter."
Economists have always analyzed the "guns versus
butter" status of every nation. So many guns have to
be made for defense, but food must also be provided
for the people. The Soviet Union has failed to do that.
They have many guns, but no butter. The same is true
for all the Soviet satellite states, including the Baltic
states of Poland, Czechoslovakia, Romania, Bulgaria,
and Yugoslavia. In going around the rim of the Soviet
Union, you will find they have all guns and no butter.
The Warsaw Pact is the strongest standing army on
earth, and their people are starving. Gorbachev
happens to be the man in power at the time when the
system has come unraveled, and according to *The
Economist* magazine of October 14, 1989, what the
Soviet Union now has is a market of 400 million
frustrated consumers. The article continues to say:

"German businessmen are swarming in to the

vacuum. Little noticed amid the excitement of the past week in Budapest and Berlin, the West German government has been busy too, pledging generous aid to help the reforms in Hungary and Poland. It is clearly set to become the biggest contributor to the bill for supporting East Europe's reformers."

This was before the crash in Eastern Europe. The last three months in 1989 saw the Berlin Wall come down, and the Soviet satellite states fall to pieces. Analysts of *The Economist* magazine stated that West Germany and others saw in 400 million frustrated consumers an incredible financial opportunity.

In introducing *glasnost* and *perestroika*, Gorbachev's motives were economic. His main incentive was to be included in the financial gains resulting from relations with the United States of Europe by 1992. He initiated reforms for the sake of economics. For example, the miners in Siberia went on strike earlier in 1990 simply because they had one slice of bread and one slice of cheese to eat *per day*! How could they work in the mines and subsist on such meager rations?

With the economic debacle in the Soviet Union, citizens demanding food, and the country itself rapidly unraveling, the Soviet Union and Eastern bloc countries are falling into the hands of the European conspiracy of the international bankers and financiers. Bankers have the money to feed, to clothe, to bring potential material wealth to 400 million frustrated consumers.

This was an opportunity for the European conspiracy to reveal itself. Gorbachev reached out to Europe. He wants the ruble to be accepted and monetized on the world market. At this time, the world bankers do not recognize the Russian currency as being worth anything. The Soviet Union will never really be accepted into the family of nations until its currency is recognized and given some kind of value. This is all Gorbachev was trying to accomplish, but what he did not realize was that he had a captive population fed up with Soviet-style communism. When they saw a crack in the communist infrastructure, they exploited it to gain their own freedom. Give a person hope, and he will go forward with great enthusiasm. When people see a small beacon of light, they mob and riot to get to that economic light.

Gorbachev is not the new, wonderful leader bringing his people into an age of utopia. What he has done is try to bring some economic reality to the Soviet Union. But the Soviet citizens do not care about him or his politics. They are hungry; they want refrigerators; they want televisions; they want cars. You can hardly blame them for what has happened in the Soviet bloc.

The people who are going to take advantage of this incredible marketing opportunity are the Germans. They are working to reunify their country, and when this process is completed, they will no longer have to rely on imported labor because they will have the labor force of East Germany. If they can reunify, Germany will be the leading country in the United States of Europe.

In continuing this study of world economics, the Bank of England has been in control of much of the world's economy for hundreds of years. Our continent was established by the Hudson Bay Company, which received financing through the Bank of England. The Bank of England helped found colonies throughout the world, which is why Great Britain owns, for example Hong Kong and the British West Indies. For hundreds of years, Europe has controlled the world economy by setting up banking systems through colonies to trade with other countries worldwide. Germany now has a very powerful economy, and the Bank of England is worried.

The French are also voicing their support for a central bank in Europe just to keep the Germans from capturing the world economic marketplace. The big story in Europe right now is the infighting between France, Germany, and England to see who is going to control world banking. It's like a giant Monopoly game with fighting around the board to see who is going to obtain control. The stakes are high — a huge untapped market, the largest market in the entire world. The one who wins will take all the marbles and in the process will receive tremendous opportunities to increase in power.

An article from the *New York Times*, January 17, 1990 says:

> *"The financial minister of France, Edward Boulladoir, has been talking up the idea of forming a European central bank in the hope of putting the matter on Western Europe's economic aid-political agenda. Many economists say French officials are vigorously calling for a European central bank because they are unhappy that West Germany, which stresses restrictive policies and anti-inflation measures far more than France, dominates the eight-nation, European monetary system"*

There are eight contending banker nations. At the moment, France is fighting Germany, and in the wings is England with the Thatcher regime. Margaret Thatcher may be in trouble right now, and some are saying the Labor Party is able to field a candidate that could become the next prime minister. If the Labor Party were to gain control of the English government, this would mean that the fight over banking in Europe would continue with increased fervor.

At the base of many of the events we see today is money. That is the mark of the beast. In the last days, people will take this mark and worship Satan, although they may not realize that this is what they are doing.

As we investigate many of the conspiratorial forces on the world scene today, often behind the scenes is evidence that those involved are Luciferians. Or are they simply men who are filled with ambition, lust, and greed? Greed blinds people to the truth of helping their fellow neighbor. Greed is probably the most likely of all to be the motivating force behind all of these events. According to the *World Book Encyclopedia*, all the wars in history have been fought over money.

In putting all of this in perspective in relation to Bible prophecy, this is a very troubling scenario, not farfetched or bizarre, but one that is very well documented. This is not an esoteric, eccentric idea. All of this relates to the fourth kingdom of Daniel, and the events in Europe could culminate in the last-days, one-world system which will propel the Antichrist to power. The United States of Europe could be the revived Holy Roman Empire, and whether it is called that or not, it could be the ten toes of Nebuchadnezzar's image in Daniel and the ten heads of Revelation 13 and 17. This developing system in Europe could bring forth the Antichrist.

While it is developing politically, the money-masters are behind the scenes jockeying for power and control. The old European monarchies are showing signs of life in Europe with the help of Otto von Habsburg and his son, Karl. There is even a great interest in Prince Charles, who will someday be the king of England, and the entire English monarchy.

All of these circumstances are like a vat of coagulating materials over a fire stirred by Satan. He is behind all of these incidents, and he is cooking a satanic stew which will eventually end in being served to mankind on the table of the last days tribulation period. Again, these are not things which are farfetched or bizarre, but they are events which a year ago people would have said could never happen.

The foundation to all of this is the mark of the beast, a world economic union and a one-world monetary system. This is the underlying motivation behind the world events happening today. All wars are fought over money and the control of it. It's all motivated by greed. The Bible says the Antichrist will demand that everyone in the world receive a mark in their right hand or forehead before they can participate in the marketplace, before they can buy or sell. It will be a controlled economy.

There is a conflict involved in the French supporting the creation of a central world bank for Europe. Once East and West Germany have reunited, East Germany will provide a great source of manpower for West Germany. The other countries in Europe are concerned. For years, West Germany has had a shrinking labor force, and Turkey has supplied cheap labor, called "guest workers." The Turkish people have enjoyed living in West Germany as "guests." In relocating to Germany, they have also brought their families and have grown in size. Demographically, German families have decreased in size. Germans are not having large families like the guest workers. The Germans are very concerned that they may lose political control to the imported guest workers. This may also have played a major role in the decision not to allow Turkey to join the European Community. With the demise of the Berlin Wall comes the possibility for West Germany to use East Germany as laborers, the guest workers would be sent back to Turkey, and all is well in the Fatherland. Germany could develop into a large, economic machine.

This is directly connected to the beast of Revelation 13. The beast was like a leopard, had the feet of a bear, the mouth of a lion, and the dragon gave him his authority. This beast looks like a leopard, not like a lion, which is the symbol for Great Britain. Great Britain is worried right now because they want to be the beast. It is very interesting that the symbol of ancient Germany was a leopard. All the nations in Europe want to be the central power in Europe, which is why their horns will be pulled up before leadership is established.

Chapter Six

The "Mark" of the Beast

by J.R. Church

Jesus is the Spirit of prophecy; His testimony is the Spirit of prophecy (Rev. 19:10). Anyone who studies prophecy receives a special blessing. In this chapter, we will examine the rise of the Antichrist, the beast, from the future revived Roman Empire.

Everything seems to be coming together to fulfill the events prophesied for the last days in the Bible. With the Berlin Wall falling, the reunification of Germany plays a very important part in the fulfillment of prophecies for the last days. The beast of Revelation 13 may have the mouth of a lion and the feet of a bear, but it looks like a leopard. The mouth of a lion possibly represents Great Britain and the role it has had over the last several hundred years. The Bank of England has established central banks in many of the world's nations and controls the economies in many nations today. Great Britain wants to be the leading economic power in the world, but the Bible pictures England only as the mouth. The body of the beast is portrayed as a leopard, possibly a German leopard. Even German tanks are called leopards. Hitler called them panthers, as in his panther divisions. Although

Hitler adopted the eagle as his symbol, the historic symbol of Germany has also been the leopard. The feet of the bear represents the Soviet republics, the Warsaw Pact nations. Four nations, one for each foot, may enter the European Community of nations before it becomes the United States of Europe in 1992.

We don't know exactly what the future holds in the next few years, but it is very probable that the battle of Gog and Magog will occur within this time period with the Soviet Union experiencing defeat in an invasion of the Middle East. One reason for this crushing debacle is because *". . . every man's sword shall be against his brother"* (Ezek. 38:21). What a magnificent picture of Soviet disintegration today!

The battle of Gog and Magog, Ezekiel 38-39, is one of the principal prophecies known to prophecy students. Among the allies of Gog and Magog, two names are specifically mentioned: Gomer and Togarmah of the north quarters. This helps us to identify what is happening today. Gomer is Germany, and Togarmah is the Baltic states, eastern regions of Poland, Czechoslavakia, Bulgaria, Yugoslavia, Turkey, and perhaps even Finland. Something strange will have to happen in the near future in order for this allegiance to unite and work together. Sometimes, discussing Gog and Magog is confusing for those who have never studied Ezekiel 38 and 39. Could these be demonic entities, cohorts of Lucifer who lead demonic forces which in turn influence men? Is there a leader named Gog and another named Magog?

The table of nations in the early chapters of Genesis helps to explain who Gog and Magog are. Magog was the son of Japheth, the Japhethites, and Togarmah was the son of Gomer. So these are not about demonic personalities but actual descendants of the peoples named specifically in the Bible. If a prophet was writing 3,000 years ago, he would use the names prevalent in the time period in which he lived. All we need to do is follow the history of these peoples to discover who they are today, and they are Germans, Romanians, Poles, Latvians, Estonians, and the balance of the Baltic and Warsaw Pact nations. All of their ancestors moved from Turkey at one time. For the Turks to move to West Germany and provide them with a labor force is not that peculiar, because the Germans descended from Turkey.

It is very important to understand that what is being studied here is an alliance of peoples. Although they may or may not be under demonic control, these nations and coalitions of major world powers of the last days are outlined in the Bible. Some think Gog and Magog are two men, or two demons working behind the scenes, so it is very important to have a clear understanding of this before we continue in our study.

Gog is a cryptic term used in Ezekiel, and no commentators, Jewish or Christian, have ever been able to translate the name from Hebrew to determine who it is. One interpretation is that Gog will surface as the leader of the Soviet Union. It is not possible to say if Mr. Gorbachev is Gog, but according to the Russian language that predates the Bolshevik Revolution, Mr. Gorbachev's family name is spelled "Gogr" instead of "Gor." Whether this has any special significance, only time will tell. When the Soviet Union invades Israel, it will be defeated because every man's sword will be against his brother as recorded in Ezekiel 38:21. This disintegration is occurring now at the heart of Soviet communism. If Mr. Gorbachev were to be pulled into a war in the Middle East today, he would certainly lose because of the deteriorating conditions within his own country. At the least, these are very intriguing observations.

What does the Bible say about Gog and military action in the last days? The prophets often made cryptic references in their prophecies for the simple reason that it is not God's plan for us to always know specific details in advance. God is working out His program, and when it is time for us to find out what He is doing, we will. Gog lives in the land of Magog, historically the land of the Scythians, which is known today as Russia, the Soviet Union. The land of Magog is described in Ezekiel 38-39 as being pulled on as if a hook were put into its jaw, drawn down into the Middle East by the power of God into a conflict which destroys the armies of Gog.

In the reference to Gog, there is also a reference

to Russia in Ezekiel 38. A fascinating discovery has been made in relation to this, and even though it has always been in the Bible, not one commentary mentions this. Commentaries have cited Rosh of Ezekiel 38:2-3, *"Son of man, set thy face against Gog, the land of Magog, the chief prince of Meschech and Tubal, and prophesy against him, And say, Thus saith the Lord God; Behold, I am against thee, O Gog, the chief prince of Meshech and Tubal."* The word "chief" in the Hebrew is *Rosh*, the Hebrew word that is today known as Russia. Theologians and commentators have written about this for years. What has been overlooked is the name of Russia mentioned by another Old Testament prophet. Jeremiah 31 describes the restoration of Israel, the regathering of the Jews from around the world. *"For thus saith the Lord; Sing with gladness for Jacob, and shout among the chief of the nations: publish ye, praise ye, and say, O Lord, save thy people, the remnant of Israel. Behold, I will bring them from the north country, and gather them from the coasts of the earth, and with them the blind and the lame, the woman with child and her that travaileth with child together: a great company shall return thither"* (Jer. 31:7-8). This is a poetic description of the regathering of the tribes of Israel. In verse 7 in the praise "chief of the nations," the word "chief" is again the word *Rosh. "Sing . . . and shout among the* [Russia] *of the nations . . . Behold, I will bring them from the north country. . . ."* The Jews are now returning to Israel from Russia, a great fulfillment of Bible prophecy.

In Ezekiel 38, God says, *"Behold, I am against thee, O Gog."* God is against this man, this power that is going to invade His holy land in the last days. Ezekiel 39:2 says, *"And I will turn thee back. . . ."* So many say that Gorbachev is a man of peace, that he has decreased the Soviet military, but that is not true — they have continued to expand strategic weaponry. They are still a strong power, perhaps the greatest conventional military power on earth today. If God already has plans to defeat the Soviet Union through its invasion of Israel, does it matter what Gorbachev wants?

For the sake of argument, let's take the position that Gorbachev actually wants peace and prosperity for his country. He is turning his back on military force. He says the Soviet Union can have peace, can have a one-world order, and can have a common European base with Russia being a part of that from the Ural mountains to the Adriatic Sea. But God has already said several thousand years ago that Russia will desire to add Israel to its conquests, perhaps even a demonic urge. Ezekiel describes it as putting *". . . hooks into thy jaws . . ."* (Ezek. 38:4). Gorbachev may not want to do any of this, he may be completely genuine. Yet something will force him to march on Israel with a military force, and evidently this will precipitate a great war and a cataclysm.

Every man's sword will be against his brother (Ezek. 38:21), and though the Soviet Union is such a potent military power, those actually doing the fighting, Russian soldiers along with those from the Warsaw Pact and other allies, are going to be divided among themselves so that Israel will be able to win this war very easily. God will do the fighting for Israel, but it will also be God who puts it in the hearts of the Russian people to rebel against their leaders. God is dismantling communism in the Soviet Union and its satellite nations in lieu of Russia's eventual bid for power in the Middle East and subsequent defeat. If the Soviet Union were united in this war effort, they certainly would present a formidable foe and possibly win. But God is preparing them to be vanquished.

It seems that on one hand the Soviet Union is apparently falling apart. There are problems in Armenia, Georgia, Latvia, Lithuania, and Azerbaidzhan. If they are falling apart, it is difficult to understand how they will have the determination and unity to invade Israel. The point is that the Soviet Union and its allies will not be united, and that will be the reason for their downfall. It is possible they might be manipulated into this war by a conflict between Israel and Syria. The next war could involve Syria, and Israel will not allow Syria to murder the Maronite Christian forces in Lebanon. For example, at this moment the Israeli government is divided and about to collapse. One way to keep the government intact and solidify unity among Israeli citizens is to turn their attention from their political strife to survival. Something may happen in Lebanon to bring about conflict between Israel and Syria. Remember, Israel does not fight half-heartedly.

Also, it is important to recall that the Warsaw Pact has not been dissolved; it is perfectly intact right now. If the Warsaw Pact nations are not involved in a war with the Soviet Union fairly soon, the Warsaw Pact itself will disband. If there were a major conflict in the Middle East, and if the Syrians found themselves in deep trouble (which would certainly happen if they attacked Israel full-scale), as Syria's principal ally, the Soviet Union would be drawn into this conflict. This is just as God prophesied through Ezekiel in the Scriptures.

But a house divided against itself cannot stand, and because Russia and its allies will not unite in the war effort, they will lose. Yet, perhaps this is why Gorbachev might consider a move to invade Israel. Gorbachev has a background in the military. He is a retired air force officer and has studied military strategy and tactics. Many wars are started because a nation has severe internal problems and dissention. In order to divert the citizenry from economic problems and social unrest and turmoil, an external power is picked as a scapegoat. This recently occurred in Iran. They had major economic problems, and the Ayatollah's solution was to go to war with Iraq. Even though Iraq precipitated the war, it united the Iranians for a time. Gorbachev might see this as a way to once more solidify his country against a common foe, the Israeli scapegoat. For centuries, the devil has influenced people to make the Jews scapegoats, and there are already strong anti-Semitic feelings within the Soviet Union. This demonic hatred of the Jews might cause some of the country to support Gorbachev in a war against Israel. He might use this as a pretext besides the oil in the Middle East also being an incentive. How much would Middle Eastern oil enrich the Russian Empire?

The ruble has not monetized, and although Gorbachev is making overtures to the European Economic Community, it is highly unlikely that this will have any effect in helping to establish Russian currency as legal tender. This might provide the impetus for Gorbachev to realize that the only way Europe is going to take the ruble seriously for use in world trade is for the Soviet Union to control the oil fields in the Middle East. As a rising world power, this might exert pressure on the European Community, and the oil could be used as a bargaining chip.

When the smoke clears, do we have the fourth beast, the beast with the body of a leopard, the feet of a bear, and the mouth of a lion with the dragon giving him authority? After the battle of Gog and Magog, will that beast present himself? It would be difficult for the leopard to develop until after the war. The leopard has the feet of a bear, and right now the bear's (Russia's) feet aren't connected to the leopard (Germany) and will not be until the demise of the Soviet Union on the northern mountains of Israel.

Recently, the chancellor of West Germany visited Berlin during the lowering of the Berlin Wall. As Helmut Kohl spoke to those in Berlin, there were cries from the crowd, "We want a fourth reich!" This is very chilling. After East and West Germany reunite, could there be a fourth reich, and could it be the basis for the kingdom of the beast? Daniel 7 describes the beast that looks like a leopard as having four heads, not three. Hitler's Third Reich must give way to a fourth reich. With its currency known as the mark, Germany will lead the way to establish a one-world currency. Some have asked what the currency of the beast will be called, the dollar, the yen, the pound, or the franc? It is possible that the common currency of the new world order will be known as the "mark." How prophetic is the wonder and majesty of Bible prophecy!

Chapter Seven

When Will the Ten Kings Receive Their Kingdoms?

by G.G. Stearman

"And the ten horns which thou sawest are ten kings, which have received no kingdom as yet; but receive power as kings one hour with the beast" (Rev. 17:12)

The astounding changes now shaking Europe seem to know no bounds. Political and economic alignments are being modified so rapidly that even seasoned observers are shaking their heads in wonder. As Europe rushes toward 1992, the announced time of unification, new leaders are waiting in the wings. Their backstage activities will soon reveal a vital new empire. Many of them are the descendants of royal families, accustomed to money, privilege, and power. Referring to the royal influence, the *London Sunday Mail* put it succinctly in a November 19, 1989 headline: "Heralding the New Age for Europe."

The paper went on to describe the sweeping changes that have stormed across Europe, and how these changes will bring new, bold leaders who will at last bring the continent to its final great destiny. Who are these leaders, and what are their goals and motives? To a very great degree, said the *Mail*, they are the sons and daughters of Europe's historical noblemen. But the fact they are royalty should come as no surprise, since the nobility has always either owned or controlled the lion's share of wealth when monarchy was in full flower.

There is every reason to believe that as Europe moves quickly toward the formation of the final great world empire, its leaders will be monarchs, in the time honored sense. They will hold great power, which they will unwittingly use to bring biblical prophecy to its final climax. In describing Europe's "new age," the *Mail* quotes Dr. Otto von Habsburg, who said:

> *"I'm certain that Hungary at least will join the European Community, and could then be followed by other East European nations, particularly Poland, although this will require lengthy and difficult negotiations. Present East European borders are likely to remain unchanged, although the Yugoslavian republic of Slovenia could break away from Yugoslavia and join the EC."*

Of course, Dr. von Habsburg is the son of Emperor Karl, last ruler of the Austro-Hungarian Empire. He, himself, has been suggested as the best candidate for the presidency of a newly-democratic

Hungary. Lately, a surprising number of news reports reflect a nostalgia for royal rule under the Habsburgs, as it manifested itself in the glory days before World War I.

In mid-November of 1989, a memorial mass was held in England for Otto's mother, the Empress Zita. She had ruled with her husband Karl for just two years, until the allied forces won in 1918. Their dynasty collapsed and they were forced to abdicate. He died, and she spent the rest of her life in exile, most lately in a Swiss monastery. 50,000 people had attended her funeral in Vienna earlier in the year.

The memorial was covered in the *London Sunday Telegram* of November 26, 1989. It began:

> *"With the brittle bones of communism becoming more exposed each day these are exciting times for the royal families of Eastern Europe and for their coterie of sometimes esoteric supporters. They live in the wings and they wait, and they watch and they wonder. Who can say now who will rule the old empire of* [Middle Europe] *so comprehensively deposed, in the year 2000?"*

The article clearly states a fact that is becoming more frequently voiced: Europe is longing for a return of strong leadership of the type once held by its monarchs. The article stated:

> *"The House of Habsburg has a more realistic*

chance — slim though it may be — of some kind of return to power in Hungary than the other deposed royal families of Eastern Europe."

The mass was conducted by Father Charles-Roux, who *"spoke for nearly half an hour about the marvels of the Holy Roman Empire."* Although not all those present publicly agreed with his sentiments, he was obviously stating the heartfelt sentiments of many within the sound of his voice. At one point, he wondered aloud about something he had recently heard. He said:

"At the European parliament six weeks ago — I forget how long but it was in the Financial Times, *a long article — who was it who proposed the re-establishment of the Holy Roman Empire? It was Otto, Otto von Habsburg and another Otto, Ott von Bismarck."*

Father Roux, in conjuring up the name of Bismarck, brought recollections of the strong leader who united the German states into one empire. He was known as the "Iron Chancellor." His famed triple alliance with Austria and Italy lasted until World War I. He was the very image of imperial power. In Europe today there seems to be a deep desire for the return of such a power.

The memorial service ended with the playing of

the Imperial National Anthem of Austria. It is the same tune to which Germans under Hitler once sang, *"Deutschland, Deutschland Uber Alles . . ."* (Germany, Germany over all). Its playing was reported as "spine-chilling and eerie."

Kings Without Kingdoms

The February 10, 1990 edition of the *London Sunday Telegraph Weekend Magazine* featured a long article entitled "Kings Without Kingdoms." Of course, the Habsburgs were prominently mentioned. Dr. von Habsburg, as usual, was described as a Bavarian Christian Democrat member of the European parliament who *"tactfully plays down imperialist fervor."* But many other potential kingdoms were mentioned, including Greece, Romania, Prussia, France, Albania, Bulgaria, Yugoslavia, Italy, and others. The writer of the report is a longtime royalty watcher named Hugh Montgomery-Massingberd. His comments are extremely interesting:

"To my mounting amazement, the New Dawn of monarchy does indeed seem to be breaking. The first dazzling glimpse of sun through the clouds came in Spain. Initially, when Juan Carlos ascended the throne in 1975 — 44 years after King Alfonso sacrificed himself to avoid bloodshed — we of little faith were ready to crack

jokes about the 'reign of Spain' and sneer at Franco's stooge. . . . In a few short years Juan Carlos dismantled the Caudillo's state and led Spain back to democracy under constitutional monarchy. . . . The Spaniards now have monarchy at its best.

"Whereas politicians can be seen, in general to be exhibitionists and careerists who are out for themselves, if not indeed corrupt crooks and tyrants, monarchs can be shown, at the very least, to be conscientious and upright; at their best, to be an inspiration to their people. Roll back the old map of Europe!"

Of course, we should remember that being British, the writer lives under a constitutional monarchy himself, and so is inclined to be prejudiced in its favor. But all over the continent, others are beginning to voice the same sentiments. There are possible prophetic implications in this rush back to monarchy. Before we look at these, let us look at some of the possibilities for restored monarchy.

Greece

Given the volatile nature of Greek politics, King Constantine has so far found his goal of establishing a constitutional monarchy too difficult to handle. Born in 1940, he ruled for only three years before being deposed in 1967 by the famed "colonel's coup." When the Greeks voted for a republic in 1974, he was officially stripped of his crown. Now living in exile in England, he is married to Princess Anne-Marie of Denmark. His sister Sophia is married to King Juan Carlos of Spain. He is said to be very serious in his efforts to return the crown to Greece.

Romania

In 1939, King Michael took the throne at the age of 19. But he was forced to abdicate when the Soviets seized his country in the aftermath of World War II. He is now 68, living in a villa on Lake Geneva in Switzerland. In the March 1990 edition of *Life* magazine, he is quoted as saying:

> *"If they want me back, of course I will go. As constitutional monarch I can guarantee them constitution, freedom, democracy. We have had this constitutional monarchy before, and I am sure it can prove itself again. The situation is a bit confusing. We have so many problems, we hardly know where to start. The main thing is to give people back their self-respect."*

This issue of *Life* features an article entitled "Kings in the Wind." It looks at a number of European monarchs who are ready, willing, and able to return to head their respective countries at a moment's notice. King Michael is poised to take over in the aftermath of the revolt against the evil Ceausescu regime. His country is now in political and economic shambles in the wake of its communist rule. Many say that the Romanian king has a good chance of coming back to pull his country out of the ashes and, in the process, bring the monarchy back to power.

Germany

Louis Ferdinand is the grandson of Kaiser Wilhelm II, who was forced to abdicate the throne of the German empire in 1918. Louis is the head of the Royal House of Hohenzollern; if there were still an empire, he would be its head. He left Germany and was an infamous Hollywood playboy in the 1930s. When he returned to Germany, he was drafted into the Luftwaffe as a pilot. But he spoke out against the Nazis, and was confined to his house in Cadinen for the duration of World War II. Now 82, he is said to have two passions: Mozart and the reunification of Germany. *Life* quoted him as saying:

"If God and the Germany people want it, I would propose a monarchy for one united Germany."

Yugoslavia

Crown Prince Alexander, son of King Peter, has

never set foot in the country once ruled by his father, King Peter II. In 1945, Alexander was born in London, and from his youth lived among the privileged classes. He is an intimate of Britain's royal family, and has made a fortune in the oil and insurance businesses.

When King Peter died in 1971, Alexander didn't take the title of king in exile, but is said to long for the *"challenge to make Yugoslavia great."* A quote from him in *Life*:

> *"I would like to see something like the Spanish monarchy, where you have a king like Juan Carlos, my cousin."*

France

Though the possibility of his ascension is remote, France also has an heir to the throne. Born in 1908, he is the Count of Paris, head of the Royal House of Bourbon-Orleans, Henri D'Orleans. He is known for an idiosyncratic personality and a great devotion to charity activity. During the 1960s, Charles DeGaulle is said to have *"toyed with the idea of re-establishing the monarchy."* Count Henri has said:

> *"The monarch is an arbiter, the incarnation of popular hope and the repository of national legitimacy."*

Albania

Known as the most repressive of all East European communist regimes, Albania's government is tottering. If it falls, King Leka will return with an enormous entourage to bring the throne back to his country. Born in 1939, the towering (6 ft., 9 in.) monarch was educated in England after fleeing the communists. In 1961, he was proclaimed king in exile. He presently resides in South Africa, and is said to be ready at a moment's notice to head for Albania. It is reported that there are more Albanian nationals living outside the country than in it, so when Leka makes his move, thousands will move with him.

Bulgaria

King Simeon II was born in 1937. His father, Boris III, died in 1943, possibly as a result of being poisoned by the Nazis. He was exiled to Egypt in 1947. There, at age 18, he said:

"I never renounced my rights to the throne."

Cautiously, he still speaks of *"the mission assigned me by providence."* King Simeon now lives in Madrid, where he runs a bureau to help exiled Bulgarians. He is said to have *"never lost faith in returning to rule his country and wants to be remembered as 'the Pacifier.'"*

Italy

Also born in 1937, Prince Victor Emmanuel is the only son of the last king of Italy. King Umberto ruled for only a month in 1946 before being defeated in a plebiscite in favor of a republic. He died in 1985. Prince Victor is a public relations man in Geneva. He has never renounced his claim to the Italian throne.

Hungary

Archduke Otto of Austria, eldest son of Karl, the last emperor of Austria and king of Hungary, prefers to be known simply as "Dr. Otto von Habsburg." Now 78, he has a long history of working toward European unification, as the president of the Pan-European Movement. During Hitler's *anschluss*, he stood firm and refused to be manipulated. Austrians still look toward him with great respect. In Hungary, which has recently adopted a democratic parliament, he is named as the most likely man for the office of president. Though he dismisses as "preposterous" the idea that he might ascend to the ancient throne, he is nevertheless a leading figure in European leadership.

More interesting still, his son Karl von Habsburg-Lothringen is a handsome and dashing law student, now aged 28. He is known as a lover of speed and adventure, as he whizzes about the scenic drives of Europe on his motorcycle, or in his Porsche 928. For several years, he has worked with his father to bring about the present move toward a United States of Europe. He has been groomed for a political career. He was recently interviewed in the April 1, 1990 issue of the German magazine, *Bunte*. When asked whether he had any serious girl friends, he answered that (because of his law studies) he had "no time." Asked about his career preference, he said simply, "politics." It is safe to say that young Karl is being groomed for an important role in tomorrow's united Europe.

These are but a few examples of Europe's possible returning monarchies. As the political map continues to change, they may well become tomorrow's rulers. Already under constitutional monarchy are the Netherlands, ruled by Queen Beatrix; Norway under King Olav; Sweden under King Carl XVI Gustaf; Denmark under Queen Margrethe II; Spain under King Juan Carlos; and England under Queen Elizabeth.

Interestingly, the Bible speaks of a latter-day group of kings who band together to form a power bloc of enormous and evil influence. Might we be seeing their assembly today?

"These Kings"

The second chapter of Daniel tells of the interpretation of the dream of King Nebuchadnezzar of Babylon. The king discovered that Daniel was able to make known the hidden meaning of dreams, so he brought him forward and told him of a dream statue with a head of gold, a chest and arms of silver, abdomen and thighs of brass, legs of iron, and feet of iron mixed with clay.

In the familiar story, Daniel tells the king that the statue is a picture of the Gentile nations down through history: Babylon is the head of gold; Medo-Persia is the chest; Greece is the abdomen of brass; Rome is the legs of iron, which terminate in ten weak toes of iron and clay. These ten toes are said to be like ten kings.

Daniel 2:42-44 says: *"And as the toes of the feet were part of iron, and part of clay, so the kingdom shall be partly strong, and partly broken. And whereas thou sawest iron mixed with miry clay, they shall mingle themselves with the seed of men: but they shall not cleave one to another, even as iron is not mixed with clay. And in the days of these kings shall the God of heaven set up a kingdom, which shall never be destroyed. . . ."*

Many times in the past, as we have read this familiar passage of Scripture, we have tended to regard this language as a metaphor. "Kings," we assumed, is simply the Bible's way of saying, "governmental leaders," whether they be presidents, prime ministers, or monarchs. Perhaps that was a false assumption. In the many scriptural references to latter-day "kings," it is possible that real ruling monarchs are being pictured. Daniel also received a vision, in which the long history of the Gentile nations was likened to four beasts, with the fourth and final beast symbolizing the Roman Empire, both in its initial and final stages. An angel, speaking to Daniel, interprets this beast in Daniel 7:23-24: *"Thus he said, The fourth beast shall be the fourth kingdom upon earth, which shall be diverse from all kingdoms, and shall devour the whole earth, and shall tread it down, and break it in pieces. And the ten horns out of this kingdom are ten kings that shall arise. . . ."* Again, Daniel tells of "ten kings." Might they be literal kings, or are they simply government leaders in general?

This beast is seen again in Revelation 13:1, as it rises out of the sea: *"And I stood upon the sand of the sea, and saw a beast rise up out of the sea, having seven heads and ten horns, and upon his horns ten crowns, and upon his heads the name of blasphemy."*

Revelation 17:12 sheds a little more light upon the beast's horns: *"And the ten horns which thou sawest are ten kings, which have received no kingdom as yet; but receive power as kings one hour with the beast."*

The great fourth and final beast is once again said to be led by "ten kings." Might we be seeing these "kings" today? As yet, they have received no kingdom, but there seems to be a great hunger for monarchy in contemporary Europe, the seat of the revived Roman Empire.

We must wait and see, but perhaps it is not premature to suggest that the ten kings of Scripture may be actual monarchs, who sit upon real thrones and give assent to the beast!

As Europe bands together into a group of states, politically and economically united to form the great power of the revived Roman Empire, there is an almost supernatural hunger being expressed for the return of monarchy. Let us watch carefully, then, to see who the final ten kings will be!

Chapter Eight

Rome Rises Again

by N.W. Hutchings

There is no more certain truth in Bible prophecy than the revival of the Roman Empire. Rome was in power when the Lord Jesus Christ came the first time, and it will again be in power when the Lord comes back the second time. For centuries, even as Europe stood hopelessly divided and embroiled in seemingly endless wars, students of prophecy have stood firm in their conviction that ten nations which were once within the geographic, political, and religious boundaries of Rome, would again form a federation of states. This federation would, in the end of the age, produce the Antichrist. It is of major importance to realize that the Common Market, according to the *New Columbia Encyclopedia*, came into being on March 25, 1957, at the invitation of Rome, and the first meeting was held in the Vatican itself. Six of the present Common Market member nations attended that first historic meeting.

The Antichrist, who will be the leader of the revived Roman Empire, will make a seven-year covenant (treaty) concerning the security of Israel (Dan. 9:27). This is a major and pivotal point in prophecy since it introduces the tribulation period, the "seventieth week of Daniel."

The noted Christian author, Dr. J.A. Seiss, foresaw the revival of Rome in conjunction with the rise of Babylon from his vantage point in history more than 130 years ago (1860). He made the following astounding observation in his book, *The Apocalypse:*

> *"Think for a moment, for there is such a power; a power that is everywhere clamouring for a common code, a common currency, common weights and measures; and which is not likely to be silenced or to stop till it has secured a common centre on its own independent basis, whence to dictate to all countries and to exercise its own peculiar rule on all the kings and nations of the earth. That power is **commerce**; the power of the ephah and the talent. . . . And when it once comes to that, as there is every prospect that it will, for Providence in judgment for the greed and covetousness of men will prosper it . . . where on earth is the spot so suited to the purpose as that where the first city this side of the flood was built? There is a great navigable river, emptying out into the open sea, whose waters have every country and island most filled with treasures of the far east. From then there are almost level avenues for railway lines to Egypt, Smyrna, and Constantinople, connecting with Vienna, Paris,*

and London . . . and which **western Europe in
its own defence will presently be compelled to
construct** *. . . thus combined without regard to
creeds or nationalities in the one great interest of
regulating and managing the commerce of the
globe, it is easy to see how every feature in the
Apocalyptic picture of Babylon would be filled
out."*

The revival of both Rome and Babylon, according
to Dr. J.A. Seiss, would be the result of economic
necessity on the part of Western Europe, and the shift
of world banking to ancient Babylon. Today, as we
see the rise of the European Economic Community
and the money surpluses of all nations being poured
into the Middle East Arab nations for oil, the
predictions made by Dr. Seiss based on Bible prophecy
are being fulfilled.

Although the following publication is several
years old, we still feel it is relevant today in the light of
Bible prophecy.

*"The European Community covers an area one-
sixth the size of the United States. Within it live
46 million more people than in the United States.
The Community members' combined gross
national product (GNP) is one-third smaller than
that of the United States. The Community is the
world's largest producer of cars and a leading*

producer of farm goods" (*Common Market* magazine, Feb. 1974).

Of course, we must remember that since this was written, Greece, Spain, and Portugal have become members of the Common Market. Europe has continued to grow economically while our growth has become stagnated.

Why was the Common Market formed? We quote from an article entitled "Why?" in the same magazine:

> *"To put an end to national prejudice, discrimination, and armed conflict which had culminated in two world wars.*
>
> *"To open up the economic frontiers which divided Western Europe into small, protected markets.*
>
> *"To harness the constructive energies of the European peoples to improve the quality of life.*
>
> *"To make the Community a single economic area, promoting social and technological progress and the efficient use of resources in both agriculture and industry.*
>
> *"To recover together some of the world influence that Western Europe's separate nations can no longer command alone.*
>
> *"To become a strong force for peace and a generous provider of aid to the world's poorer*

nations.

"*To contribute to world stability and the beginnings of international law and order.*"

Of course, the first items are very important and if they had not formed the Common Market, these nations of Europe would have remained in a weak and impoverished condition. The Common Market was necessary if Europe was to exist. According to Daniel 11, in the end of the age the Gentile nations will be divided into four main power blocs:

1. King of the North — Russia
2. King of the South — Egypt and the African nations
3. King of the East — China and the nations of the Orient
4. King of the West — revived Rome of Western Europe

The prophetic picture concerning the rise of a powerful ten-nation alliance in the end of the age out of the old Roman Empire begins in the second chapter of Daniel. King Nebuchadnezzar of ancient Babylon had visions of establishing a dynasty that would last forever. God revealed to him, in a dream, the course of the Gentile nations, until God's own King would come from Heaven. God's revelation of future history to Nebuchadnezzar was in the form of an image.

According to the prophecy, the head of gold on the image represented ancient Babylon. However, the prophecy also foretold that Babylon would fall to a two-part empire represented by the breast and two arms of silver. The conqueror of Babylon proved to be the Medo-Persian Empire. The prophecy also revealed that Medo-Persia would then fall to another empire — Greece rose up and conquered Medo-Persia. However, Greece was consumed by an even greater empire — this empire was represented by the two legs of iron on the image. This fourth world empire is described in Daniel 2:40-42, 44: *"And the fourth kingdom shall be strong as iron: forasmuch as iron breaketh in pieces and subdueth all things: and as iron that breaketh all these, shall it break in pieces and bruise. And whereas thou sawest the feet and toes, part of potters' clay, and part of iron, the kingdom shall be divided; but there shall be in it of the strength of iron, forasmuch as thou sawest the iron mixed with miry clay. And as the toes of the feet were part of iron, and part of clay, so the kingdom shall be partly strong, and partly broken. . . . And in the days of these kings shall the God of heaven set up a kingdom, which shall never be destroyed: and the kingdom shall not be left to other people, but it shall break in pieces and consume all these kingdoms, and it shall stand forever."*

The Word of God concerning the future of nations reveals that the Roman Empire would be broken into pieces, but when ten of the pieces formed an alliance at the end of the age, then the world would know that the coming of the Messiah to establish His own kingdom over the earth would be near.

Rome appeared as a world power in 242 B.C. with the conquest of Sicily. Gradually, the iron law of Rome was extended westward to Spain, northward to Germany and England, and eastward to Egypt and Syria. The Roman army under General Pompeius took protective custody of Jerusalem in 63 B.C., completing the replacement of Greece as the dominant world empire. The dominion of Rome over its conquered territories was as brittle and unyielding as iron in every respect. Taxes, goods, slaves, and produce flooded the markets of Rome from all over the known world. The citizens of Rome lived like kings while the rest of the world lived like paupers. All roads led to Rome. Daniel, by the inspiration of God, said, *"And the fourth kingdom shall be strong as iron: forasmuch as iron breaketh in pieces and subdueth all things: and as iron that breaketh all these, shall it break in pieces and bruise"* (Dan. 2:40).

In the chronological order of world empires, Rome, "the iron kingdom," broke into pieces, with each piece becoming a nation. Rome has never ceased to exist; it simply broke up into independent nations, and all dictatorships today can trace their governmental structure back to Rome. As the two legs of iron represented Rome, the empire was divided into two parts — the western division with Rome as its capital, and the eastern division with Constantinople as the capital. The two legs stood side by side as one empire until the iron empire began to break up in the year A.D. 476. The break occurred first in the right leg. The position of nations according to the Bible is as they face Jerusalem. In A.D. 773, Charlemagne became emperor of the Holy Roman Empire, and though he tried to heal the split, he never quite succeeded. In the year A.D. 963 Italy was overrun by Germany, a province that Rome had difficulty keeping under subjection. The Germans absorbed the western division of Rome and moved the capital to Berlin. The Germans then claimed the throne of the Roman Empire, and they named their king "kaiser," which is German for "caesar."

The eastern division of Rome, and especially the southern part, gradually succumbed to rising Arab nationalism as promoted by Mohammed from A.D. 570 to A.D. 632. On his first military campaign into Asia Minor, Mohammed brought back 3,000 Christian idols to Mecca. The churches of Asia did not heed God's warning issued in Revelation chapters 2 and 3, and their candlesticks were removed. However, the capital of the eastern division of Rome was not conquered until A.D. 1453 by Mohammed II.

The Russians conquered and annexed much of the northern half of the eastern division of Rome, including Armenia. One historical source notes that Russians even occupied Constantinople for a time, and established St. Petersburg as the capital of eastern Rome. Eventually the capital was transferred to Moscow where it remains today. The Russians named their ruler "czar," which is Russian for "caesar." The Bolshevik Revolution, which was taken over by the communists, replaced the government of the Russian caesars by a system of commissars, or communist caesars. The board of communist caesars in Russia is presided over by a high caesar, and the present chairman of the board is Mikhail Gorbachev.

The relationship of the so-called "free world" with communism has gone through a series of changes — from allies, to direct confrontation, to peaceful coexistence, to detente, and now to *glasnost*. The liberal propaganda has been that communism would mellow and change to a more yielding socialistic form of political ideology. But Russia is one of the iron pieces in the leg of the Gentile image, and iron cannot change its shape except it be melted down and recast. The very symbols of communism are iron: the iron hammer, the iron sickle, and the iron fist.

Daniel prophesied almost 2,500 years ago that the Roman Empire would break into pieces and bruise, and the prophet said the bruising would occur when anyone attempted to put the pieces together again. There have indeed been many such attempts, and as prophesied in the Bible, constant wars and bloodshed have resulted. The two greatest wars the world has ever known, World Wars I and II, began between nations of the old Roman Empire trying to put the image back together. But before World War I, numerous attempts were made, and one of the most notable of these was made by Napoleon. Napoleon conquered all the western leg of Rome with the exception of England, and the emperor overran all the eastern leg of Rome with the exception of Moscow. He did occupy Moscow for a time, but he was not able to hold it. It was in Russia that he suffered a humiliating defeat from which his dreams for reuniting Rome never recovered. His vision was ultimately shattered at the battle of Waterloo in 1815, and history records that Napoleon's final defeat was due to an act of God. It simply was not time on God's prophetic calendar for Rome to be revived as the kingdom of the Antichrist.

After Napoleon, the next most serious attempt to weld together the pieces of iron was made by the kaiser, or caesar of Germany in World War I. Then came World War II when Adolf Hitler of Germany and Benito Mussolini of Italy formed the Axis Alliance. Adolf Hitler made the same mistake that Napoleon made. He struck east at the old eastern leg of Rome while leaving England, an unconquered portion of the western leg, and the United States, at his rear.

After World War II, Russia, which still possessed the relocated capital of eastern Rome, was presented with a golden opportunity also to capture the relocated capital of western Rome, Berlin. But Berlin stands as the sole example of where the United States has constantly resisted communist pressure. It is reported that after World War II, Eisenhower had to threaten to use the atomic bomb against Russia in order to obtain the partitioning of Berlin. In this dividing of the city, the old capital buildings and sites remained in possession of the Allies instead of Russia. In spite of constant communist pressure, including the Berlin blockade, the United States has stood firm. In May of 1975, Henry Kissinger, then Secretary of State, went to Berlin to make a speech affirming the resolve of the United States to hold the German capital, even in the face of war.

Chapter Nine

The Parade of Four Beasts

by N.W. Hutchings

In accordance with the pre-written history of the Roman Empire in Daniel 2, Rome broke up into individual nations beginning with the fifth century A.D. In spite of numerous attempts at reunification from the time of Charlemagne to Adolf Hitler, the wars of Europe only resulted in massive bruisings without accomplishing their intended purpose. However, with each attempt to reform the empire, a clearer picture of what will actually happen during the reign of Antichrist was presented. In the alliance of Hitler and Mussolini, a type of the union between the "political beast" and the "religious beast" of Revelation 13 appeared. Hitler became the greatest persecutor of the Jews ever to arise, and he even branded identification numbers on the forearms of the Jews. World War II lasted for six years (1939 to 1945), nearly the length of time given for the tribulation period. Hitler sent his armies into North Africa to attempt the conquest of Jerusalem and the land of Palestine, and in this he almost succeeded. According to Bible prophecy, Hitler could have become the Antichrist, and those ministers during World War II who sounded the

98

alarm that great signs concerning the soon return of Jesus Christ were in evidence, are to be commended rather than condemned.

However, we notice that the revival of Rome, as depicted in Daniel, is not to come about through war, but rather through a union of federated states. In the extremity of the toes on the Gentile image, the iron pieces are to remain separated and be mixed with clay when the Antichrist appears. As many Bible scholars have pointed out, in contrasting the clay with iron as relating to governments, the iron signifies military dictatorships and the clay represents democratic states, and even more likely, socialism, as we approach the end of the age.

It is also important to our study to keep in mind that world power does not lie in Washington, D.C., Moscow, or Peking. World power is now centered in the Common Market of Europe, where it has been for the past 2,000 years. Germany, fighting virtually alone, has almost conquered the world twice in one generation. Napoleon of France built the greatest army the world had seen to that time. If Europe had not been divided, Napoleon would have become a world ruler. The same is true of Kaiser Wilhelm and Adolf Hitler.

Nevertheless, the cohesive force to hold the iron pieces of Rome together has been economics. Marxism, which evolved into communism, came out of Germany through Karl Marx. Frederic Bastiat in 1848, in his book *The Law*, projected that communism and socialism from Europe would engulf the earth unless there was a return to the basic laws of God set forth in the Ten Commandments.

From the most western nation of the old Roman Empire, England, socialism has spread as fast as Marxism did in Germany. The June 1975 edition of *Reader's Digest*, in an article entitled "The United States and the New World Society," made the following observation:

"*The notion of a world society is nothing new to America. . . . But there is something new in international pronouncements. . . . It is almost as if American opinion now acknowledged that there was no escaping involvement in the emergent world society. What happened in the early 1970s is that for the first time the world felt the impact of what I shall call the British revolution which began in 1947 with the granting by socialist Britain of independence to socialist India. In slow, then rapid order, the great empires of the world — with the major exception of the former czarist empire — broke up into independent states; the original U.N. membership of 51 grew to 138 . . . socialist doctrine as it developed in Britain was that it was anti-American. More anti-American, surely, than it was ever anti-Soviet. . . . In the first half of the 20th century, British*

*civil servants took the doctrine of British socialism
to the colonies, a domain which covered one
quarter of the earth's surface. By 1950 not
communists but Fabian socialists could claim
that the largest portion of the world's population
lived in regimes of their fashioning. . . ."*

The pieces which broke off the iron nation of
Rome have indeed mixed with miry clay in the end of
the age just prophesied. The United States finds itself
in an emerging world society of socialism. As the
author of the article in *Reader's Digest* suggests, our
country is being carried along with the tide of our
times to a new one-world order which has emerged
through the economic and political policies which
have risen in Western Europe over the last century.
One of the foremost organizations in our country
which has directed this nation to that end is the
Council on Foreign Relations.

The Common Market of Europe is not a new
idea. It is simply an extension of the trade agreements
which have kept the old Roman Empire together since
the fifth century. A cookbook published by Doubleday
on the history of food from ancient times to modern
times had this to say about the Common Market of
Europe:

*"Fairs and markets were the light side of the
Dark Ages and focal points of the burgeoning*

*international economy. Caravans of merchants,
minstrels, and peasants met seasonally to display
and sell products ranging from songs and salted
meats to rare spices and silks. Most famous were
the fairs of Champagne near Paris held in the
twelfth and thirteenth centuries. They lasted
anywhere from sixteen to fifty days."*

At the fairs and markets of Europe, princes and
kings would meet to negotiate trade agreements.
Naturally, political and religious matters entered into
the deliberations. The revival of the Common Market
of Europe today indicates the resumption of the old
idea that if Rome is to be put back together again, it
will be accomplished through peaceful economic
cooperation rather than by military means. The
sowing of the seeds of socialism and communism,
both one-world political ideologies, has set the stage
for the revived Roman Empire to reap the harvest.
The competition and controvery among the main four
blocs of nations is only setting the stage for Rome
again to rule the world.

In Daniel 7 we are given a description of four
great world empires. These empires are called "beasts"
because they devour much flesh. *"Daniel spake and
said, I saw in my vision by night, and, behold, the four
winds of the heaven strove upon the great sea. And
four great beasts came up from the sea, diverse one
from another"* (Dan. 7:2-3).

The Mediterranean Sea in the Scriptures is called the "great sea." As Daniel looked upon the sea, the four winds of heaven began to blow. The violent storm awakened four dormant monsters which came forth to prowl upon the earth, and all four beasts were predators — flesh-eating animals. Because the setting for this prophecy is in the night, it concerns the night of great tribulation. Winds are symbolic of spirit forces, and in the latter days it is predicted in the Bible that Satan would unleash devils and stir up the nations to war and rebellion against God (Rev. 16:12-14).

We read more about these four beast empires in Daniel 7:4-8: *"The first was like a lion, and had eagle's wings: I beheld till the wings thereof were plucked, and it was lifted up from the earth, and made stand upon the feet as a man, and a man's heart was given to it. And behold another beast, a second, like to a bear, and it raised up itself on one side, and it had three ribs in the mouth of it between the teeth of it: and they said thus unto it, Arise, devour much flesh. After this I beheld, and lo another, like a leopard, which had upon the back of it four wings of a fowl; the beast had also four heads; and dominion was given to it. After this I saw in the night visions, and behold a fourth beast, dreadful and terrible, and strong exceedingly; and it had great iron teeth: it devoured and brake in pieces, and stamped the residue with the feet of it: and it was diverse from all the beasts that were before it;*

and it had ten horns. I considered the horns, and, behold, there came up among them another little horn, before whom there were three of the first horns plucked up by the roots: and, behold, in this horn were eyes like the eyes of man, and a mouth speaking great things.''

The common interpretation of Daniel 7 is that the prophecy of the four beasts refers to the successive empires of Babylon, Medo-Persia, Greece, and Rome, as depicted in the Gentile world image of Daniel 2. However, we call your attention to Daniel 7:17, *"These great beasts, which are four, are four kings, which shall arise out of the earth."* When Daniel interpreted the dream of Nebuchadnezzar concerning the image of Daniel 2, he pointed to the king of Babylon and said, *"Thou, O king, art the head of gold."* There was no question at all about Babylon's being the first empire represented in the image. But in regard to the four beasts of Daniel 7, the prophet said that from his vantage point in history, these predatory animals representing four empires would arise in the future. Therefore, Babylon could not have been included as one of the beasts, because Babylon was a world empire at that time. It seems evident from the setting for the prophecy of the four beasts that it is in the latter years, the last generation of the age. It concerns four empires that will have vital interests in the Mediterranean area.

The first beast to appear is described as a lion with

eagle's wings. The emblem of England is a lion, and the national emblem of the United States is an eagle. The Anglo-Saxon world of America and England ruled the Mediterranean from 1918 to 1968. England ruled from 1918 to 1948, and the United States from 1948 to 1968, when Russia began to gain superiority over the Mediterranean Sea. The second beast is described as a bear, the well-known emblem of Russia. And, in accordance with the prophecy, Russia succeeded England and the United States as the predominant power in the Mediterranean Sea. The shift in the balance of power came in 1968 when the strength of the Soviet fleet began to exceed that of the U.S. 6th Fleet in the Great Sea.

The third beast is described as a leopard with four wings on its back, and it gains some measure of power over the Middle East through delegated authority. We read that dominion will be given unto it. According to Ezekiel 38 and 39, Russia will be defeated either just before, or immediately after the tribulation period begins and the communist hordes invade Israel. Thereafter, Russian influence in the Middle East is bound to decline or be eliminated altogether. The "leopard empire" is depicted as becoming dominant in the Mediterranean between the exit of the bear and the appearance of the fourth and dreadful beast. The leopard was adopted by the emerging African nations as their emblem for nationalism. We remember that the Mau Mau terrorists of Africa, who were in the forefront of the African nationalist movement, used leopard skins and claws in their attacks upon colonial rule and authority. The wings on the back of the leopard indicate delegated and protective authority from an outside source, possibly the United Nations. We quote again from the article, "The United States and the New World Order," from the June 1975 edition of *Reader's Digest:*

> " '*We are now witnessing the emergence of a world order domination arithmetically by the countries of the Third World,*' *writes Daniel P. Moynihan, former U.S. Ambassador to India. . . . Increasingly, the United States stands 'accused and abased' before these nations. . . . While often hostile, these nations are not communist; generally, they are socialist. To date, their ideology has had limited force but, in the General Assembly of the United Nations and a dozen other such international forums, this new majority will set about to legislate 'its presumed advantage in a world that has just come into its hands.*' "

This article continues to present the proposition that through the United Nations a new force to be reckoned with has come into being — the Afro-Asian bloc that controls the United Nations. It is entirely possible that such a bloc of nations could rule the Mediterranean Sea area between the defeat of Russian armed forces upon the mountains of Israel (Ezek. 38) and the rise of the kingdom of Antichrist out of the revived Roman Empire. The leopard is also a traditional symbol for Germany, and as of this date is is a foregone conclusion that West Germany and East Germany will be reunited as one nation. Prospects for the new Germany are already reviving old fears in Europe and in Israel. An AP news release dated February 20, 1990, was headlined, "Reunification Speech Stirs Jewish Fears." Rev. J.R. Church believes that Germany will join with Russia in accordance with Ezekiel 38:6 in an invasion of Israel.

We now come to the final Gentile authority in the Middle East and the Mediterranean area before Christ returns, the great and terrible beast with iron teeth and ten horns. The great majority of pre-millennial Bible authorities identify this beast as the revived Roman Empire. The iron teeth identify the beast empire as an extension of Rome, and the ten horns stand for ten rulers who will be aligned with the Antichrist. It is the fourth empire that constitutes the kingdom of Antichrist, and it will conquer the whole earth after the defeat of Russia in Israel. Out of the ten nations from the Roman Empire a president will arise to rule over the federation.

The following information is taken from the *European Economic Community* magazine, May 1979:

"Right now, 410 carefully elected representatives

from nine European countries are discussing the problems of the world. Their decisions could affect everyone on earth. Who is this select group? The new parliament of the European Common Market, jostling to become a world power. The Common Market is already the world's largest trading bloc, importing and exporting more than the United States and the Soviet Union combined. It has a population of 270 million, and a gross domestic product almost as large as the United States. January 1, the Common Market will add Greece as its tenth member. Already the accession agreement has been signed and the formal process of parliamentary ratification is taking place. As the Greek foreign minister put it, Greece will be an equal member of a huge democratic society of 270 million, with a political voice equal to that of the major European powers in the decision-making process."

According to the prophecy in Daniel 7, the Antichrist will remove three of the rulers of the ten nations in his federation. Perhaps these three will rebel against his plans to make himself the object of worship of all nations when he reveals himself as the Antichrist. We read of the scope of his empire in Daniel 7:23-25: *". . . The fourth beast shall be the fourth kingdom upon earth, which shall be diverse from all kingdoms, and shall devour the whole earth, and shall tread it down, and break it in pieces. And the ten horns out of this kingdom are ten kings that shall arise: and another shall rise after them; and he shall be diverse from the first, and he shall subdue three kings. And he shall speak great words against the most High, and shall wear out the saints of the most High, and think to change times and laws: and they shall be given into his hand until a time and times and the dividing of time* [three and a half years according to Jewish reckoning of time]."

The corresponding prophecy in Revelation 13:6-10 informs us that during the three and a half years, the dictator of the beast empire rules over all the earth, he will demand that all the inhabitants of the world worship him as God. All who refuse will be killed.

Chapter Ten

Israel and the Three Beasts

by N.W. Hutchings

Concerning the setting of the stage for the reappearing of the Lord, there is a most interesting prophecy in Amos 5:18-20, *"Woe unto you that desire the day of the Lord! to what end is it for you? the day of the Lord is darkness, and not light. As if a man did flee from a lion, and a bear met him; or went into the house, and leaned his hand on the wall, and a serpent bit him. Shall not the day of the Lord be . . . ?"* The preceding prophecy by Amos was, of course, meant for Israel. The day of the Lord referred to by the prophet is the coming of Israel's Messiah to fulfill the promises made to Abraham, Isaac, and Jacob. Amos, as well as all the other prophets, warned that the day of the Lord would not come except it were preceded by a time of sorrow, woe, and trouble. For example, it is declared in Joel 1:15, *"Alas for the day! for the day of the Lord is at hand, and as a destruction from the Almighty shall it come."* Jesus said that in the day He would come again to Israel, there would be a time of trouble such as the world had never seen (Matt. 24:21).

However, in returning to the prophecy of Amos,

it is noted by the prophet that Israel would be looking for the day of the Lord without knowing that a great time of trouble must first come. So Amos compared the troubles of Israel in the last days to a man who, while running from a lion, met a bear. The lion was frightened off by the bear, but then the bear took up the chase. In order to get away from the bear, the man ran into his house and shut the door. Exhausted, he put his hand on the wall to steady himself, and a snake bit him.

This prophetic analogy by Amos is an accurate and penetrating description of the plight of the Jews in the last days. As we have brought out before, agressor nations have grown into empires by absorbing other nations, and this is the reason predatory beasts are chosen as emblems for empires. According to Amos, the first beast to be encountered by the refounded nation of Israel before the day of the Lord would be a lion. After World War I, the land of Palestine became a British protectorate. In spite of the Balfour Declaration, Jewish immigration was restricted to a few thousand a year. Hitler's persecution of the Jews during World War II accelerated their return to the land after the war ended. Because the chief promoter of a new Jewish state after World War II was Russia, it was assumed by England and the United States that the new nation would become a communist beachhead in Africa. British warships patrolled the Mediterranean Sea, turning back vessels carrying Jewish refugees, and armed patrols guarded the beaches. Meanwhile, U.S. diplomats at the United Nations were busily engaged mustering political support in an attempt to prevent Israel from becoming a sovereign state. The Jewish people appealed directly to President Harry Truman, and the president demanded that all efforts against the refounding of Israel as a nation be stopped. In 1948, the United Nations voted to accept Israel as a nation, and Great Britain gave way. As Amos prophesied, Israel escaped from the clutches of the lion. The emblem of England is a lion.

However, after escaping the lion, Amos prophesied that Israel would meet a bear. Joseph Stalin learned a basic Bible truth the hard way. He learned that once a Jew returns to the land of Palestine, he is no longer a Russian, an American, a German, or a citizen of any other nation. Once he is back in the land, a Jew becomes an Israelite. Some contend that Russia backed the Jews' return to the land only because the communist leaders in Moscow knew that trouble would occur between Israel and the Arab nations, and by taking the side of the Arabs, Russia could take over the oil-rich Middle East. Whether this is true or not is open to question. In any event, the fact remains that all these things have happened in accordance with Bible prophecy; and according to Ezekiel 38 and 39, Russia will join with a large segment of the Arab world in a final attempt to annihilate Israel. The army of Gog mentioned in

Ezekiel 38:1-6 that will come against Israel in the latter years is that of Russia. Every reliable commentary identifies Gog as Russia, and Russia is even called Gog in Israeli newspapers. Israel accepts, in an almost fatalistic attitude, that at some future time Russia will make an attempt to destroy the Jewish state.

God has stated quite plainly in Ezekiel 38 that Russia will launch a military invasion of Israel just prior to the day of the Lord. The emblem of Russia is a bear. Amos prophesied that after Israel escaped from the lion, she would meet a bear. However, Ezekiel 39:21-23 states that the Russian army will be destroyed upon the mountains of Israel. God will intervene and permit Israel to escape the bear.

After escaping the bear, Israel will become safe and secure in her own land. However, the prophecy continues to relate that the Jews will be bitten by a serpent in their own house. The serpent that will bite Israel is identified in Revelation 13:4, *"And they* [the unsaved world] *worshipped the dragon which gave power unto the beast: and they worshipped the beast, saying, Who is like unto the beast? who is able to make war with him?"* We also read of the serpent in Revelation 12:9, *". . . the great dragon . . . that old serpent, called the Devil, and Satan. . . ."*

The serpent is the biblical emblem of Satan and the Antichrist. According to Daniel 9:27, the Antichrist will make a treaty with Israel for seven years, guaranteeing Israel's right to the land for that length of time. After three and a half years, the deceitful serpent will break the treaty. The fact that Israel will be bitten by the serpent in her own house is further proof that the Antichrist will be a Jew by race — one of his own house.

In Daniel 9:26 the prophet referred to the coming destruction of Jerusalem, *". . . and the people of the prince that shall come shall destroy the city and the sanctuary. . . ."* After the demise of Nero by suicide to escape public trial, several men attempted to rule the empire, but they were weak or more corrupt than Nero. Finally, the senate recalled General Vespasian from his command in Israel. Before Vespasian left for Rome, the general put his own son, Captain Titus, in charge of the army. As the Roman army made its final assault against Jerusalem, breached the walls, and destroyed the Temple, Vespasian reigned as caesar, making his son, Titus, a prince, thus fulfilling Daniel's prophecy in every detail. However, the importance of this prophecy to our day is that the man who will make a covenant with Israel, the Antichrist, will come from the people of the prince who destroyed Jerusalem and the Temple, or the revived Roman Empire.

Another item of interest in Daniel's prophecy relating to the events leading up to the covenant with Antichrist and the abomination of desolation is that *"the end thereof shall come with a flood."* Events in Europe and Russia in the latter half of 1989 and the first half of 1990 have transpired so rapidly, it is as one news commentator remarked

> *"It seems that God has placed history on fast-forward."*

Besides the Eastern European nations gaining sudden freedom from communist domination in order that they might fulfill their prophetic destiny, a new rise in anti-Semitism is gaining momentum, accelerating the return of the Jews from Russia to Israel. President George Bush toppled the Israeli government with a remark indicating that the United States has changed its position on East Jerusalem.

Iraq (ancient Babylon) is caught attempting to smuggle atomic bomb parts through England. President Assad of Syria calls for a new and total "holy war" against Israel. The Energy Commission in early 1990 warned that an expected energy crisis will arrive before 1995, making Middle East oil more precious and desirable to all nations, especially Russia.

Bible prophecy in Daniel 7:24 and Revelation 17:12 clearly states that the Antichrist kingdom will be ruled over by ten kings. Today in the Common Market alliance of Europe there are three royal heads who reign over monarchial democracies: Queen Elizabeth, of England; Queen Julianna, of the Netherlands; and King Juan Carlos, of Spain. But as Gary Stearman brings out in chapter seven, there are ten royal heads in Europe today who are without thrones. Due to the rapid changes that have occurred in Europe in 1989 and 1990, they are hoping to regain their thrones. Admittedly, some seem to have only a slight chance, but considering the turn of events this past year which previously not even seasoned political observers would have dared to predict, it is not impossible deposed kings and queens will regain their thrones.

In Nebuchadnezzar's dream in Daniel 2, the gold in the image's head represented King Nebuchadnezzar. The declining metals represented monarchial systems of less power. In the feet of the image from which the Antichrist kingdom will come, small pieces of iron are mixed with clay, telling us that in the revived Roman Empire the kings will be weak and subservient to the people, much like the Queen of England. This is what appears to be developing in Europe today, and of this time we read in Daniel 2:44, *"And in the days of these kings shall the God of heaven set up a kingdom, which shall never be destroyed: and the kingdom shall not be left to other people, but it shall break in pieces and consume all these kingdoms, and it shall stand for ever."*

Christians today are privileged to be living in exciting, thrilling days. If Jesus Christ were to come today for His church, would you, the reader, be ready?